DE QUINCEY'S WRITINGS.

It is the intention of the publishers to issue, at intervals, a complete collection of Mr. De Quincey's Writings, uniform with this volume. The first four volumes of the series contain, —

I. Confessions of an English Opium-Eater and Suspiria De Profundis.

II. Biographical Essays.

III. Miscellaneous Essays.

IV. The Cæsars.

Following these will appear the Autobiography, originally published in Tait's Magazine, — and the Sketches of Literary Men, including Wordsworth, Coleridge, Southey, Lamb and others, collected from various sources.

MISCELLANEOUS ESSAYS.

BY

THOMAS DE QUINCEY,

AUTHOR OF

CONFESSIONS OF AN ENGLISH OPIUM-EATER,' ETC. ETC

BOSTON:
TICKNOR, REED, AND FIELDS.
M DCCC LI.

THURSTON, TORRY, AND EMERSON, PRINTERS.

CONTENTS.

MISCELLANEOUS ESSAYS.

ON

THE KNOCKING AT THE GATE

IN MACBETH.

From my boyish days I had always felt a great perplexity on one point in Macbeth. It was this : the knocking at the gate, which succeeds to the murder of Duncan, produced to my feelings an effect for which I never could account. The effect was, that it reflected back upon the murder a peculiar awfulness and a depth of solemnity ; yet, however obstinately I endeavored with my understanding to comprehend this, for many years I never could see *why* it should produce such an effect.

Here I pause for one moment, to exhort the reader never to pay any attention to his understanding, when it stands in opposition to any other faculty of his mind. The mere understanding, however useful and indispensable, is the meanest faculty in the human mind, and the most to be distrusted; and yet the great majority of people trust to nothing else; which may do for ordinary life, but not for philosophical purposes. Of this out of ten thousand instances that I might produce, I will cite one. Ask of any person whatsoever, who is not previously prepared for the demand by a knowledge of perspective, to draw in the rudest way the commonest appearance which depends upon the laws of that science; as, for instance, to represent the effect of two walls standing at right angles to each other, or the appearance of the houses on each side of a street, as seen by a person looking down the street from one extremity. Now in all cases, unless the person has happened to observe in pictures how it is that artists produce these effects, he will be utterly unable to make the smallest approximation to it. Yet why? For he has actually seen the effect every day of his life. The reason is — that he allows his understanding to overrule his eyes. His understanding, which includes no intuitive knowledge of the laws of vision, can furnish him with no reason why a line which is known and can be proved to be a horizontal line, should not *appear* a horizontal line; a line that made any angle with the perpendicular, less than a right angle, would seem to him to indicate that his houses were all tumbling down together. Accordingly, he makes the line of his houses a horizontal line, and fails, of course, to produce the effect demanded. Here, then, is one instance out of many, in which not only the understanding is allowed to overrule the eyes, but where the understanding is positively allowed to obliterate the eyes, as it were, for not only does the man believe the evidence of his understanding, in opposition to that of his eyes, but, (what is monstrous !) the idiot is not aware that his eyes ever gave such evidence. He does not know that he has seen (and therefore *quoad* his consciousness has *not* seen) that which he *has* seen every day of his life.

But to return from this digression, my understanding could furnish no reason why the knocking at the gate in Macbeth, should produce any effect, direct or reflected. In fact, my understanding said positively that it could *not* produce any effect. But I knew better ; I felt that it did ; and I waited and clung to the problem until further knowledge should enable me to solve it. At length, in 1812, Mr. Williams made his *début* on the stage of Ratcliffe Highway, and executed those unparalleled murders which have procured for him such a brilliant and undying reputation. On which murders, by the way, I must observe, that in one respect they have had an ill effect, by making the connoisseur in murder very fastidious in his taste, and dissatisfied by anything that has been since done in that line. All other murders look pale by the deep crimson of his ; and, as an amateur once said to me in a querulous tone, 'There has been absolutely nothing *doing* since his time, or nothing that 's worth speaking of.' But this is wrong ; for it is unreasonable to expect all men to be great artists, and born with the genius of Mr. Williams. Now it will be remembered, that in the first of these murders, (that of the Marrs,) the same incident (of a knocking at the door, soon after the work of extermination was complete) did actually occur, which the genius of Shakspeare has invented; and all good judges, and the most eminent dilettanti, acknowledged the felicity of Shakspeare's suggestion, as soon as it was actually realized. Here, then, was a fresh proof that I was right in relying on my own feeling, in opposition to my understanding; and I again set myself to study the problem; at length I solved it to my own satisfaction; and my solution is this. Murder, in ordinary cases, where the sympathy is wholly directed to the case of the murdered person, is an incident of coarse and vulgar horror; and for this reason, that it flings the interest exclusively upon the natural but ignoble instinct by which we cleave to life; an instinct, which, as being indispensable to the primal law of self-preservation, is the same in kind, (though different in degree,) amongst all living creatures; this instinct, therefore, because it annihilates all distinctions, and degrades the greatest of men to the level of "the poor beetle that we tread on," exhibits human nature in its most abject and humiliating attitude. Such an attitude would little suit the purposes of the poet. What then must he do? He must throw the interest on the murderer. Our sympathy must be with *him*; (of course I mean a sympathy of comprehension, a sympathy by which we enter into his feelings, and are made to understand them, — not a sympathy[1] of pity

[1] It seems almost ludicrous to guard and explain my use of a word, in a situation where it would naturally explain itself. But it has become necessary to do so, in consequence of the unscholarlike use of the word sympathy, at present so general, by which, instead of taking it in its proper sense, as the act of

or approbation.) In the murdered person, all strife of thought, all flux and reflux of passion and of purpose, are crushed by one overwhelming panic; the fear of instant death smites him 'with its petrific mace.' But in the murderer, such a murderer as a poet will condescend to, there must be raging some great storm of passion, — jealousy, ambition, vengeance, hatred, — which will create a hell within him; and into this hell we are to look.

In Macbeth, for the sake of gratifying his own enormous and teeming faculty of creation, Shakspeare has introduced two murderers: and, as usual in his hands, they are remarkably discriminated: but, though in Macbeth the strife of mind is greater than in his wife, the tiger spirit not so awake, and his feelings caught chiefly by contagion from her, — yet, as both were finally involved in the guilt of murder, the murderous mind of necessity is finally to be presumed in both. This was to be expressed; and on its own account, as well as to make it a more proportionable antagonist to the unoffending nature of their victim, 'the gracious Duncan,' and adequately to expound 'the deep damnation of his taking off,' this was to be expressed with peculiar energy. We were to be made to feel that the human nature, *i. e.*, the divine nature of love and mercy, spread through the hearts of all creatures, and seldom utterly

---

reproducing in our minds the feelings of another, whether for hatred, indignation, love, pity, or approbation, it is made a mere synonyme of the word *pity;* and hence, instead of saying 'sympathy *with* another,' many writers adopt the monstrous barbarism of 'sympathy *for* another.'

withdrawn from man, — was gone, vanished, extinct; and that the fiendish nature had taken its place. And, as this effect is marvellously accomplished in the *dialogues* and *soliloquies* themselves, so it is finally consummated by the expedient under consideration; and it is to this that I now solicit the reader's attention. If the reader has ever witnessed a wife, daughter, or sister, in a fainting fit, he may chance to have observed that the most affecting moment in such a spectacle, is *that* in which a sigh and a stirring announce the recommencement of suspended life. Or, if the reader has ever been present in a vast metropolis, on the day when some great national idol was carried in funeral pomp to his grave, and chancing to walk near the course through which it passed, has felt powerfully, in the silence and desertion of the streets, and in the stagnation of ordinary business, the deep interest which at that moment was possessing the heart of man, — if all at once he should hear the death-like stillness broken up by the sound of wheels rattling away from the scene, and making known that the transitory vision was dissolved, he will be aware that at no moment was his sense of the complete suspension and pause in ordinary human concerns so full and affecting, as at that moment when the suspension ceases, and the goings-on of human life are suddenly resumed. All action in any direction is best expounded, measured, and made apprehensible, by reaction. Now apply this to the case in Macbeth. Here, as I have said, the retiring of the human heart, and the entrance of the fiendish heart, was to be expressed and made sensible. Another world has stept in; and the murderers are taken out of the region of human things, human purposes, human desires. They are transfigured: Lady Macbeth is 'unsexed;' Macbeth has forgot that he was born of woman; both are conformed to the image of devils; and the world of devils is suddenly revealed. But how shall this be conveyed and made palpable? In order that a new world may step in, this world must for a time disappear. The murderers, and the murder, must be insulated — cut off by an immeasurable gulph from the ordinary tide and succession of human affairs — locked up and sequestered in some deep recess; we must be made sensible that the world of ordinary life is suddenly arrested — laid asleep — tranced — racked into a dread armistice: time must be annihilated; relation to things without abolished; and all must pass self-withdrawn into a deep svncope and suspension of earthly passion. Hence it is, that when the deed is done, when the work of darkness is perfect, then the world of darkness passes away like a pageantry in the clouds: the knocking at the gate is heard; and it makes known audibly that the reaction has commenced: the human has made its reflux upon the fiendish; the pulses of life are beginning to beat again; and the re-establishment of the goings-on of the world in which we live, first makes us profoundly sensible of the awful parenthesis that had suspended them.

O, mighty poet! Thy works are not as those of other men, simply and merely great works of art; but are also like the phenomena of nature, like the sun and the sea, the stars and the flowers, — like frost and snow, rain and dew, hail-storm and thunder, which are to be studied with entire submission of our own faculties, and in the perfect faith that in them there can be no too much or too little, nothing useless or inert — but that, the further we press in our discoveries, the more we shall see proofs of design and self-supporting arrangement where the careless eye had seen nothing but accident!

ON MURDER,

CONSIDERED AS ONE OF THE FINE ARTS.

TO THE EDITOR OF BLACKWOOD'S MAGAZINE.

SIR, — We have all heard of a Society for the Promotion of Vice, of the Hell-Fire Club, &c. At Brighton, I think it was, that a Society was formed for the Suppression of Virtue. That society was itself suppressed — but I am sorry to say that another exists in London, of a character still more atrocious. In tendency, it may be denominated a Society for the Encouragement of Murder; but, according to their own delicate ευφημισμὸς, it is styled — The Society of Connoisseurs in Murder. They profess to be curious in homicide; amateurs and dilettanti in the various modes of bloodshed; and, in short, Murder-Fanciers. Every fresh atrocity of that class, which the police annals of Europe bring up, they meet and criticise as they would a picture, statue, or other work of art. But I need not trouble myself with any attempt to describe the spirit of their proceedings, as you will collect *that* much better from one of the Monthly Lectures read before the society last year. This has fallen into my hands accidentally, in spite of all the vigilance exercised to keep their transactions from the public eye. The publication of it will alarm them; and my purpose is that it should. For I would much rather put them down quietly, by an appeal to public opinion through you, than by such an exposure of names as would follow an appeal to Bow Street; which last appeal, however, if this should fail, I must positively resort to. For it is scandalous that such things should go on in a Christian land. Even in a heathen land, the toleration of murder was felt by a Christian writer to be the most crying reproach of the public morals. This writer was Lactantius; and with his words, as singularly applicable to the present occasion, I shall conclude: 'Quid tam horribile,' says he, 'tam tetrum, quam hominis trucidatio? Ideo severissimis legibus vita nostra munitur; ideo bella execrabilia sunt. Invenit tamen consuetudo quatenus homicidium sine bello ac sine legibus faciat: et hoc sibi voluptas quod scelus vindicavit. Quod si interesse homicidio sceleris conscientia est, — et eidem facinori spectator obstrictus est cui et admissor; ergo et in his gladiatorum cædibus non minus cruore profunditur qui spectat, quam ille qui facit: nec potest esse immunis à sanguine qui voluit effundi; aut videri non interfecisse, qui interfectori et favit et prœmium postulavit.' 'Human life,' says he, 'is guarded by laws of the uttermost rigor, yet custom has devised a mode of evading them in behalf of murder; and the demands of taste (voluptas) are now become the same as those of abandoned guilt.' Let the Society of Gentlemen Amateurs consider this; and let me call their especial attention to the last sentence, which is so weighty, that I shall attempt to convey it in English: 'Now, if merely to be present at a murder fastens on a man the character of an accomplice; if barely to be a spectator involves us in one common guilt with the perpetrator; it follows of necessity, that, in these murders of the amphitheatre, the hand which inflicts the fatal blow is not more deeply imbrued in blood than his who sits and looks on: neither can *he* be clear of blood who has countenanced its shedding; nor that man seem other than a participator in murder who gives his applause to the murderer, and calls for prizes in his behalf.' The '*præmia postulavit*' I have not yet heard charged upon the Gentlemen Amateurs of London, though undoubtedly their proceedings tend to that; but the '*interfectori favit*' is implied in the very title of this association, and expressed in every line of the lecture which I send you.

I am, &c. X. Y. Z.

LECTURE.

Gentlemen, — I have had the honor to be appointed by your committee to the trying task of reading the Williams' Lecture on Murder, considered as one of the Fine Arts; a task which might be easy enough three or four centuries ago, when the art was little understood, and few great models had been exhibited; but in this age, when masterpieces of excellence have been executed by professional men, it must be evident, that in the style of criticism applied to them, the public will look for something of a corresponding improvement. Practice and theory must advance *pari passu.*

People begin to see that something more goes to the composition of a fine murder than two blockheads to kill and be killed — a knife — a purse — and a dark lane. Design, gentlemen, grouping, light and shade, poetry, sentiment, are now deemed indispensable to attempts of this nature. Mr. Williams has exalted the ideal of murder to all of us; and to me, therefore, in particular, has deepened the arduousness of my task. Like Æschylus or Milton in poetry, like Michael Angelo in painting, he has carried his art to a point of colossal sublimity; and, as Mr. Wordsworth observes, has in a manner 'created the taste by which he is to be enjoyed.' To sketch the history of the art, and to examine its principles critically, now remains as a duty for the connoisseur, and for judges of quite another stamp from his Majesty's Judges of Assize.

Before I begin, let me say a word or two to certain prigs, who affect to speak of our society as if it were in some degree immoral in its tendency. Immoral! God bless my soul, gentlemen, what is it that people mean? I am for morality, and always shall be, and for virtue and all that; and I do affirm, and always shall, (let what will come of it,) that murder is an improper line of conduct, highly improper; and I do not stick to assert, that any man who deals in murder, must have very incorrect ways of thinking, and truly inaccurate principles; and so far from aiding and abetting him by pointing out his victim's hiding-place, as a great moralist[1] of Germany declared it to be

[1] Kant — who carried his demands of unconditional veracity to so extravagant a length as to affirm, that, if a man were to see an innocent person escape from a murderer, it would be his

every good man's duty to do, I would subscribe one shilling and sixpence to have him apprehended, which is more by eighteen-pence than the most eminent moralists have subscribed for that purpose. But what then? Everything in this world has two handles. Murder, for instance, may be laid hold of by its moral handle, (as it generally is in the pulpit, and at the Old Bailey;) and *that*, I confess, is its weak side; or it may also be treated *æsthetically*, as the Germans call it, that is, in relation to good taste.

To illustrate this, I will urge the authority of three eminent persons, viz., S. T. Coleridge, Aristotle, and Mr. Howship the surgeon. To begin with S. T. C. One night, many years ago, I was drinking tea with him in Berners' Street, (which, by the way, for a short street, has been uncommonly fruitful in men of genius.) Others were there besides myself; and amidst some carnal considerations of tea and toast, we were all imbibing a dissertation on Plotinus from the attic lips of S. T. C. Suddenly a cry arose of '*Fire—fire!*' upon which all of us, master and disciples, Plato and όι περὶ τον Πλάτωνα, rushed out, eager for the spectacle. The fire was in Oxford Street, at a piano-forte maker's; and, as it promised to be a conflagration of merit, I was sorry that my engagements forced me away from Mr. Coleridge's party before matters were come to a

---

duty, on being questioned by the murderer, to tell the truth, and to point out the retreat of the innocent person, under any certainty of causing murder. Lest this doctrine should be supposed to have escaped him in any heat of dispute, on being taxed with it by a celebrated French writer, he solemnly reaffirmed it, with his reasons.

crisis. Some days after, meeting with my Platonic host, I reminded him of the case, and begged to know how that very promising exhibition had terminated. 'Oh, Sir,' said he, 'it turned out so ill, that we damned it unanimously.' Now, does any man suppose that Mr. Coleridge, — who, for all he is too fat to be a person of active virtue, is undoubtedly a worthy Christian, — that this good S. T. C., I say, was an incendiary, or capable of wishing any ill to the poor man and his piano-fortes (many of them, doubtless, with the addional keys)? On the contrary, I know him to be that sort of man, that I durst stake my life upon it he would have worked an engine in a case of necessity, although rather of the fattest for such fiery trials of his virtue. But how stood the case? Virtue was in no request. On the arrival of the fire-engines, morality had devolved wholly on the insurance office. This being the case, he had a right to gratify his taste. He had left his tea. Was he to have nothing in return?

I contend that the most virtuous man, under the premises stated, was entitled to make a luxury of the fire, and to hiss it, as he would any other performance that raised expectations in the public mind, which afterwards it disappointed. Again, to cite another great authority, what says the Stagyrite? He (in the Fifth Book, I think it is, of his Metaphysics) describes what he calls κλεπτὴν τέλειον, i. e., *a perfect thief;* and, as to Mr. Howship, in a work of his on Indigestion, he makes no scruple to talk with admiration of a certain ulcer which he had seen, and which he styles 'a beautiful ulcer.' Now will any man pretend, that, abstractedly considered, a thief could appear to Aristotle a perfect character, or that Mr. Howship could be enamored of an ulcer? Aristotle, it is well known, was himself so very moral a character, that, not content with writing his Nichomachéan Ethics, in one volume octavo, he also wrote another system, called *Magna Moralia*, or Big Ethics. Now, it is impossible that a man who composes any ethics at all, big or little, should admire a thief *per se*, and, as to Mr. Howship, it is well known that he makes war upon all ulcers; and, without suffering himself to be seduced by their charms, endeavors to banish them from the county of Middlesex. But the truth is, that, however objectionable *per se*, yet, relatively to others of their class, both a thief and an ulcer may have infinite degrees of merit. They are both imperfections, it is true; but to be imperfect being their essence, the very greatness of their imperfection becomes their perfection. *Spartam nactus es, hanc exorna.* A thief like Autolycus or Mr. Barrington, and a grim phagedænic ulcer, superbly defined, and running regularly through all its natural stages, may no less justly be regarded as ideals after *their* kind, than the most faultless moss-rose amongst flowers, in its progress from bud to 'bright consummate flower;' or, amongst human flowers, the most magnificent young female, apparelled in the pomp of womanhood. And thus not only the ideal of an inkstand may be imagined, (as Mr. Coleridge demonstrated in his celebrated correspondence with Mr. Blackwood,) in which, by the way, there is not so much, because an inkstand is a laudable sort of thing, and a valuable member of society; but even imperfection itself may have its ideal or perfect state.

Really, gentlemen, I beg pardon for so much philosophy at one time, and now let me apply it. When a murder is in the paulo-post-futurum tense, and a rumor of it comes to our ears, by all means let us treat it morally. But suppose it over and done, and that you can say of it, Τετέλεσται, or (in that adamantine molossus of Medea) εἴργασται; suppose the poor murdered man to be out of his pain, and the rascal that did it off like a shot, nobody knows whither; suppose lastly, that we have done our best, by putting out our legs to trip up the fellow in his flight, but all to no purpose — 'abiit, evasit,' &c. — why, then, I say, what's the use of any more virtue? Enough has been given to morality; now comes the turn of Taste and the Fine Arts. A sad thing it was, no doubt, very sad; but *we* can't mend it. Therefore let us make the best of a bad matter; and, as it is impossible to hammer anything out of it for moral purposes, let us treat it æsthetically, and see if it will turn to account in that way. Such is the logic of a sensible man, and what follows? We dry up our tears, and have the satisfaction, perhaps, to discover that a transaction, which, morally considered, was shocking, and without a leg to stand upon, when tried by principles of Taste, turns out to be a very meritorious performance. Thus all the world is pleased; the old proverb is justified, that it is an ill wind which blows nobody good; the amateur, from looking bilious and sulky, by too close an attention to virtue, begins to pick up his crumbs, and general hilarity prevails. Virtue has had her day; and henceforward, *Vertu* and Connoisseurship have leave to provide for themselves. Upon this principle, gentlemen, I propose to guide your studies, from Cain to Mr. Thurtell. Through this great gallery of murder, therefore, together let us wander hand in hand, in delighted admiration, while I endeavor to point your attention to the objects of profitable criticism.

The first murder is familiar to you all. As the inventor of murder, and the father of the art, Cain must have been a man of first-rate genius. All the Cains were men of genius. Tubal Cain invented tubes, I think, or some such thing. But, whatever were the originality and genius of the artist, every art was then in its infancy, and the works must be criticised with a recollection of that fact. Even Tubal's work would probably be little approved at this day in Sheffield; and therefore of Cain (Cain senior, I mean) it is no disparagement to say, that his performance was but so so. Milton, however, is supposed to have thought differently. By his way of relating the case, it should seem to have been rather a pet murder with him, for he retouches it with an apparent anxiety for its picturesque effect:

> Whereat he inly raged; and, as they talk'd,
> Smote him into the midriff with a stone
> That beat out life: he fell; and, deadly pale,
> Groan'd out his soul *with gushing blood effus'd*.
>
> *Par. Lost, B. XI.*

Upon this, Richardson, the painter, who had an eye for effect, remarks as follows, in his Notes on Paradise Lost, p. 497: 'It has been thought,' says he, 'that Cain beat (as the common saying is) the breath out of

3

his brother's body with a great stone; Milton gives in to this, with the addition, however, of a large wound.' In this place it was a judicious addition; for the rudeness of the weapon, unless raised and enriched by a warm, sanguinary coloring, has too much of the naked air of the savage school; as if the deed were perpetrated by a Polypheme without science, premeditation, or anything but a mutton bone. However, I am chiefly pleased with the improvement, as it implies that Milton was an amateur. As to Shakspeare, there never was a better; as his description of the murdered Duke of Gloucester, in Henry VI., of Duncan's, Banquo's, &c., sufficiently proves.

The foundation of the art having been once laid, it is pitiable to see how it slumbered without improvement for ages. In fact, I shall now be obliged to leap over all murders, sacred and profane, as utterly unworthy of notice, until long after the Christian era. Greece, even in the age of Pericles, produced no murder of the slightest merit; and Rome had too little originality of genius in any of the arts to succeed, where her model failed her. In fact, the Latin language sinks under the very idea of murder. 'The man was murdered;'— how will this sound in Latin? *Interfectus est*, *interemptus est* — which simply expresses a homicide; and hence the Christian Latinity of the middle ages was obliged to introduce a new word, such as the feebleness of classic conceptions never ascended to. *Murdratus est*, says the sublimer dialect of Gothic ages. Meantime, the Jewish school of murder kept alive whatever was yet known in the art, and gradually transferred it to the Western World. Indeed the Jewish school was always respectable, even in the dark ages, as the case of Hugh of Lincoln shows, which was honored with the approbation of Chaucer, on occasion of another performance from the same school, which he puts into the mouth of the Lady Abbess.

Recurring, however, for one moment to classical antiquity, I cannot but think that Catiline, Clodius, and some of that coterie, would have made first-rate artists; and it is on all accounts to be regretted, that the priggism of Cicero robbed his country of the only chance she had for distinction in this line. As the *subject* of a murder, no person could have answered better than himself. Lord! how he would have howled with panic, if he had heard Cethegus under his bed. It would have been truly diverting to have listened to him; and satisfied I am, gentlemen, that he would have preferred the *utile* of creeping into a closet, or even into a *cloaca*, to the *honestum* of facing the bold artist.

To come now to the dark ages — (by which we, that speak with precision, mean, *par excellence*, the tenth century, and the times immediately before and after) — these ages ought naturally to be favorable to the art of murder, as they were to church architecture, to stained glass, &c.; and, accordingly, about the latter end of this period, there arose a great character in our art, I mean the Old Man of the Mountains. He was a shining light, indeed, and I need not tell you, that the very word 'assassin' is deduced from him. So keen an amateur was he, that on one occasion, when his own life was attempted by a favorite assassin, he was so much pleased with the talent shown, that notwithstanding the failure of the artist, he created him a duke upon the spot, with remainder to the female line, and settled a pension on him for three lives. Assassination is a branch of the art which demands a separate notice ; and I shall devote an entire lecture to it. Meantime, I shall only observe how odd it is, that this branch of the art has flourished by fits. It never rains, but it pours. Our own age can boast of some fine specimens ; and, about two centuries ago, there was a most brilliant constellation of murders in this class. I need hardly say, that I allude especially to those five splendid works, — the assassinations of William I., of Orange, of Henry IV., of France, of the Duke of Buckingham, (which you will find excellently described in the letters published by Mr. Ellis, of the British Museum,) of Gustavus Adolphus, and of Wallenstein. The King of Sweden's assassination, by the by, is doubted by many writers, Harte amongst others ; but they are wrong. He was murdered ; and I consider his murder unique in its excellence ; for he was murdered at noon-day, and on the field of battle, — a feature of original conception, which occurs in no other work of art that I remember. Indeed, all of these assassinations may be studied with profit by the advanced connoisseur. They are all of them *exemplaria*, of which one may say, —

Nocturnâ versatâ manu, versate diurne ;

Especially *nocturnâ*.

In these assassinations of princes and statesmen, there is nothing to excite our wonder; important changes often depend on their deaths ; and, from the eminence on which they stand, they are peculiarly exposed to the aim of every artist who happens to be possessed by the craving for scenical effect. But there is another class of assassinations, which has prevailed from an early period of the seventeenth century, that really *does* surprise me; I mean the assassination of philosophers. For, gentlemen, it is a fact, that every philosopher of eminence for the two last centuries has either been murdered, or, at the least, been very near it; insomuch, that if a man calls himself a philosopher, and never had his life attempted, rest assured there is nothing in him; and against Locke's philosophy in particular, I think it an unanswerable objection, (if we needed any,) that, although he carried his throat about with him in this world for seventy-two years, no man ever condescended to cut it. As these cases of philosophers are not much known, and are generally good and well composed in their circumstances, I shall here read an excursus on that subject, chiefly by way of showing my own learning.

The first great philosopher of the seventeenth century (if we except Galileo) was Des Cartes; and if ever one could say of a man that he was all *but* murdered — murdered within an inch — one must say it of him. The case was this, as reported by Baillet in his *Vie De M. Des Cartes*, tom. I. p. 102–3. In the year 1621, when Des Cartes might be about twenty-six years old, he was touring about as usual, (for he was as restless as a hyæna,) and, coming to the Elbe, either at Gluckstadt or at Hamburgh, he took shipping for East Friezland: what he could want in East Friezland no man has ever discovered; and perhaps he took this into consideration himself; for, on reaching Embden, he resolved to sail instantly for *West* Friezland; and being very impatient of delay, he hired a bark, with a few mariners to navigate it. No sooner had he got out to sea than he made a pleasing discovery, viz., that he had shut himself up in a den of murderers. His crew, says M. Baillet, he soon found out to be 'des scélérats,' — not *amateurs*, gentlemen, as we are, but professional men — the height of whose ambition at that moment was to cut his throat. But the story is too pleasing to be abridged; I shall give it, therefore, accurately, from the French of his biographer: 'M. Des Cartes had no company but that of his servant, with whom he was conversing in French. The sailors, who took him for a foreign merchant, rather than a cavalier, concluded that he must have money about him. Accordingly they came to a resolution by no means advantageous to his purse. There is this difference, however, between sea-robbers and the robbers in forests, that the latter may, without hazard, spare the lives of their victims; whereas the other cannot put a passenger on shore in such a case without running the risk of being apprehended. The crew of M. Des Cartes arranged their measures with a view to evade any danger of that sort. They observed that he was a stranger from a distance, without acquaintance in the country, and that nobody would take any trouble to inquire about him, in case he should never come to hand, (*quand il viendroit à manquer*.') Think, gentlemen, of these Friezland dogs discussing a philosopher as if he were a puncheon of rum. 'His temper, they remarked, was very mild and patient; and, judging from the gentleness of his deportment, and the courtesy with which he treated themselves, that he could be nothing more than some green young man, they concluded that they should have all the easier task in disposing of his life. They made no scruple to discuss the whole matter in his presence, as not supposing that he understood any other language than that in which he conversed with his servant; and the amount of their deliberation was — to murder him, then to throw him into the sea, and to divide his spoils.'

Excuse my laughing, gentlemen, but the fact is, I always *do* laugh when I think of this case — two things about it seem so droll. One is, the horrid panic or 'funk,' (as the men of Eton call it,) in which Des Cartes must have found himself upon hearing this regular drama sketched for his own death — funeral — succession and administration to his effects. But another thing, which seems to me still more funny about this affair is, that if these Friezland hounds had been 'game,' we should have no Cartesian philosophy; and how we could have done without *that*, considering the world of books it has produced, I leave to any respectable trunk-maker to declare.

However, to go on; spite of his enormous funk, Des Cartes showed fight, and by that means awed these Anti-Cartesian rascals. 'Finding,' says M. Baillet, 'that the matter was no joke, M. Des Cartes leaped upon his feet in a trice, assumed a stern countenance that these cravens had never looked for, and addressing them in their own language, threatened to run them through on the spot if they dared to offer him any insult.' Certainly, gentlemen, this would have been an honor far above the merits of such inconsiderable rascals — to be spitted like larks upon a Cartesian sword; and therefore I am glad M. Des Cartes did not rob the gallows by executing his threat, especially as he could not possibly have brought his vessel to port, after he had murdered his crew; so that he must have continued to cruise for ever in the Zuyder Zee, and would probably have been mistaken by sailors for the *Flying Dutchman*, homeward bound. 'The spirit which M. Des Cartes manifested,' says his biographer, 'had the effect of magic on these wretches. The suddenness of their consternation struck their minds with a confusion which blinded them to their advantage, and they conveyed him to his destination as peaceably as he could desire.'

Possibly, gentlemen, you may fancy that, on the model of Cæsar's address to his poor ferryman,—'*Cæsarem vehis et fortunas ejus*,' — M. Des Cartes needed only to have said, — 'Dogs, you cannot cut my throat, for you carry Des Cartes and his philosophy,' and might safely have defied them to do their worst. A German emperor had the same notion, when, being cautioned to keep out of the way of a cannonading, he replied, 'Tut! man. Did you ever hear of a cannon-ball that killed an emperor?' As to an emperor I cannot say, but a less thing has sufficed to smash a philosopher; and the next great philosopher of Europe undoubtedly *was* murdered. This was Spinosa.

I know very well the common opinion about him is, that he died in his bed. Perhaps he did, but he was murdered for all that; and this I shall prove by a book published at Brussels, in the year 1731, entitled, *La Via de Spinosa; Par M. Jean Colerus*, with many additions, from a MS. life, by one of his friends. Spinosa died on the 21st February, 1677, being then little more than forty-four years old. This, of itself, looks suspicious; and M. Jean admits, that a certain expression in the MS. life of him would warrant the conclusion, 'que sa mort n' a pas été tout-à-fait naturelle.' Living in a damp country, and a sailor's country, like Holland, he may be thought to have indulged a good deal in grog, especially in punch,[1] which was then newly discovered. Undoubtedly he might have done so; but the fact is, that he did not. M. Jean calls him 'extrêmement sobre en son boire et en son manger.' And though some wild stories were afloat about his using the juice of mandragora, (p. 140,) and opium, (p. 144,) yet neither of these articles appeared in his druggist's bill. Living, therefore, with such sobriety, how was it possible that he should die a natural death at forty-four? Hear his biographer's account:—'Sunday morning, the 21st of February, before it was church time, Spinosa came down stairs and conversed with the master and mistress of the house.' At this time, therefore, perhaps ten o'clock on Sunday morning, you see that Spinosa was alive, and pretty well. But it seems 'he

---

[1] 'June 1, 1675.—Drinke part of 3 boules of punch, (a liquor very strainge to me,)' says the Rev. Mr. Henry Teonge, in his Diary lately published. In a note on this passage, a reference is made to Fryer's Travels to the East Indies, 1672, who speaks of 'that enervating liquor called *Paunch,* (which is Indostan for five,) from five ingredients.' Made thus, it seems the medical men called it Diapente; if with four only, Diatessaron. No doubt, it was its Evangelical name that recommended it to the Rev. Mr. Teonge.

had summoned from Amsterdam a certain physician, whom,' says the biographer, 'I shall not otherwise point out to notice than by these two letters, L. M. This L. M. had directed the people of the house to purchase an ancient cock, and to have him boiled forthwith, in order that Spinosa might take some broth about noon, which in fact he did, and ate some of the *old cock* with a good appetite, after the landlord and his wife had returned from church.

'In the afternoon, L. M. staid alone with Spinosa, the people of the house having returned to church; on coming out from which, they learnt, with much surprise, that Spinosa had died about three o'clock, in the presence of L. M., who took his departure for Amsterdam the same evening, by the night-boat, without paying the least attention to the deceased. No doubt he was the readier to dispense with these duties, as he had possessed himself of a ducatoon, and a small quantity of silver, together with a silver-hafted knife, and had absconded with his pillage.' Here you see, gentlemen, the murder is plain, and the manner of it. It was L. M. who murdered Spinosa for his money. Poor S. was an invalid, meagre, and weak: as no blood was observed, L. M., no doubt, threw him down and smothered him with pillows, — the poor man being already half suffocated by his infernal dinner. But who was L. M.? It surely never could be Lindley Murray; for I saw him at York, in 1825; and besides, I do not think he would do such a thing; at least, not to a brother grammarian: for you know, gentlemen, that Spinosa wrote a very respectable Hebrew grammar.

Hobbes, but why, or on what principle, I never could

understand, was not murdered. This was a capital oversight of the professional men in the seventeenth century; because in every light he was a fine subject for murder, except, indeed, that he was lean and skinny; for I can prove that he had money, and (what is very funny,) he had no right to make the least resistance; for, according to himself, irresistible power creates the very highest species of right, so that it is rebellion of the blackest die to refuse to be murdered, when a competent force appears to murder you. However, gentlemen, though he was not murdered, I am happy to assure you that (by his own account) he was three times very near being murdered. The first time was in the spring of 1640, when he pretends to have circulated a little MS. on the king's behalf, against the Parliament; he never could produce this MS., by the by; but he says that, 'Had not his Majesty dissolved the Parliament,' (in May,) 'it had brought him into danger of his life.' Dissolving the Parliament, however, was of no use; for, in November of the same year, the Long Parliament assembled, and Hobbes, a second time, fearing he should be murdered, ran away to France. This looks like the madness of John Dennis, who thought that Louis XIV. would never make peace with Queen Anne, unless he were given up to his vengeance; and actually ran away from the sea-coast in that belief. In France, Hobbes managed to take care of his throat pretty well for ten years; but at the end of that time, by way of paying court to Cromwell, he published his Leviathan. The old coward now began to 'funk' horribly for the third time; he fancied the swords of the cavaliers were constantly at his throat, recollecting how they had served the Parliament ambassadors at the Hague and Madrid. 'Tum,' says he, in his dog-Latin life of himself,

> 'Tum venit in mentem mihi Dorislaus et Ascham;
> Tanquam proscripto terror ubique aderat.'

And accordingly he ran home to England. Now, certainly, it is very true that a man deserved a cudgelling for writing Leviathan; and two or three cudgellings for writing a pentameter ending so villanously as — 'terror ubique aderat!' But no man ever thought him worthy of anything beyond cudgelling. And, in fact, the whole story is a bounce of his own. For, in a most abusive letter which he wrote 'to a learned person,' (meaning Wallis the mathematician,) he gives quite another account of the matter, and says (p. 8,) he ran home 'because he would not trust his safety with the French clergy;' insinuating that he was likely to be murdered for his religion, which would have been a high joke indeed — Tom's being brought to the stake for religion.

Bounce or not bounce, however, certain it is, that Hobbes, to the end of his life, feared that somebody would murder him. This is proved by the story I am going to tell you: it is not from a manuscript, but (as Mr. Coleridge says) it is as good as manuscript; for it comes from a book now entirely forgotten, viz. 'The Creed of Mr. Hobbes Examined; in a Conference between him and a Student in Divinity,' (published about ten years before Hobbes's death.) The book is anonymous, but it was written by Tennison, the same who, about thirty years after, succeeded Tillotson as

Archbishop of Canterbury. The introductory anecdote is as follows: 'A certain divine, it seems, (no doubt Tennison himself,) took an annual tour of one month to different parts of the island. In one of these excursions (1670) he visited the Peak in Derbyshire, partly in consequence of Hobbes's description of it. Being in that neighborhood, he could not but pay a visit to Buxton; and at the very moment of his arrival, he was fortunate enough to find a party of gentlemen dismounting at the inn door, amongst whom was a long thin fellow, who turned out to be no less a person than Mr. Hobbes, who probably had ridden over from Chattsworth. Meeting so great a lion, — a tourist, in search of the picturesque, could do no less than present himself in the character of bore. And luckily for this scheme, two of Mr. Hobbes's companions were suddenly summoned away by express; so that, for the rest of his stay at Buxton, he had Leviathan entirely to himself, and had the honor of bowsing with him in the evening. Hobbes, it seems, at first showed a good deal of stiffness, for he was shy of divines; but this wore off, and he became very sociable and funny, and they agreed to go into the bath together. How Tennison could venture to gambol in the same water with Leviathan, I cannot explain; but so it was: they frolicked about like two dolphins, though Hobbes must have been as old as the hills; and 'in those intervals wherein they abstained from swimming and plunging themselves,' [i. e. diving,] 'they discoursed of many things relating to the Baths of the Ancients, and the Origine of Springs. When they had in this manner passed away an hour, they stepped out of the bath; and, having dried and cloathed themselves, they sate down in expectation of such a supper as the place afforded; designing to refresh themselves like the *Deipnosophilæ*, and rather to reason than to drink profoundly. But in this innocent intention they were interrupted by the disturbance arising from a little quarrel, in which some of the ruder people in the house were for a short time engaged. At this Mr. Hobbes seemed much concerned, though he was at some distance from the persons.' And why was he concerned, gentlemen? No doubt you fancy, from some benign and disinterested love of peace and harmony, worthy of an old man and a philosopher. But listen—'For a while he was not composed, but related it once or twice as to himself, with a low and careful tone, how Sextus Roscius was murthered after supper by the Balneæ Palatinæ. Of such general extent is that remark of Cicero, in relation to Epicurus the Atheist, of whom he observed that he of all men dreaded most those things which he contemned—Death and the Gods.' Merely because it was supper time, and in the neighborhood of a bath, Mr. Hobbes must have the fate of Sextus Roscius. What logic was there in this, unless to a man who was always dreaming of murder? Here was Leviathan, no longer afraid of the daggers of English cavaliers or French clergy, but 'frightened from his propriety' by a row in an ale-house between some honest clod-hoppers of Derbyshire, whom his own gaunt scare-crow of a person that belonged to quite another century, would have frightened out of their wits.

Malebranche, it will give you pleasure to hear, was

murdered. The man who murdered him is well known: it was Bishop Berkeley. The story is familiar, though hitherto not put in a proper light. Berkeley, when a young man, went to Paris and called on Père Malebranche. He found him in his cell cooking. Cooks have ever been a *genus irritabile;* authors still more so: Malebranche was both: a dispute arose; the old father, warm already, became warmer; culinary and metaphysical irritations united to derange his liver: he took to his bed, and died. Such is the common version of the story: 'So the whole ear of Denmark is abused.' The fact is, that the matter was hushed up, out of consideration for Berkeley, who (as Pope remarked) had 'every virtue under heaven:' else it was well known that Berkeley, feeling himself nettled by the waspishness of the old Frenchman, squared at him; a *turn-up* was the consequence: Malebranche was floored in the first round; the conceit was wholly taken out of him; and he would perhaps have given in; but Berkeley's blood was now up, and he insisted on the old Frenchman's retracting his doctrine of Occasional Causes. The vanity of the man was too great for this; and he fell a sacrifice to the impetuosity of Irish youth, combined with his own absurd obstinacy.

Leibnitz, being every way superior to Malebranche, one might, *a fortiori*, have counted on *his* being murdered; which, however, was not the case. I believe he was nettled at this neglect, and felt himself insulted by the security in which he passed his days. In no other way can I explain his conduct at the latter end of his life, when he chose to grow very avaricious, and to hoard up large sums of gold, which he kept in his own house. This was at Vienna, where he died; and letters are still in existence, describing the immeasurable anxiety which he entertained for his throat. Still his ambition, for being *attempted* at least, was so great, that he would not forego the danger. A late English pedagogue, of Birmingham manufacture, viz., Dr. Parr, took a more selfish course, under the same circumstances. He had amassed a considerable quantity of gold and silver plate, which was for some time deposited in his bed-room at his parsonage house, Hatton. But growing every day more afraid of being murdered, which he knew that he could not stand, (and to which, indeed, he never had the slightest pretension,) he transferred the whole to the Hatton blacksmith; conceiving, no doubt, that the murder of a blacksmith would fall more lightly on the *salus reipublicæ*, than that of a pedagogue. But I have heard this greatly disputed; and it seems now generally agreed, that one good horse-shoe is worth about $2\frac{1}{4}$ Spital sermons.

As Leibnitz, though not murdered, may be said to have died, partly of the fear that he should be murdered, and partly of vexation that he was not, — Kant, on the other hand — who had no ambition in that way — had a narrower escape from a murderer than any man we read of, except Des Cartes. So absurdly does fortune throw about her favors! The case is told, I think, in an anonymous life of this very great man. For health's sake, Kant imposed upon himself, at one time, a walk of six miles every day along a highroad. This fact becoming known to a man who had his private reasons for committing murder, at the third milestone from Königsberg, he waited for his 'intended,' who came up to time as duly as a mail-coach.

But for an accident, Kant was a dead man. However, on considerations of 'morality,' it happened that the murderer preferred a little child, whom he saw playing in the road, to the old transcendentalist: this child he murdered; and thus it happened that Kant escaped. Such is the German account of the matter; but my opinion is — that the murderer was an amateur, who felt how little would be gained to the cause of good taste by murdering an old, arid, and adust metaphysician; there was no room for display, as the man could not possibly look more like a mummy when dead, than he had done alive.

Thus, gentlemen, I have traced the connection between philosophy and our art, until insensibly I find that I have wandered into our own era. This I shall not take any pains to characterize apart from that which preceded it, for, in fact, they have no distinct character. The seventeenth and eighteenth centuries, together with so much of the nineteenth as we have yet seen, jointly compose the Augustan age of murder. The finest work of the seventeenth century is, unquestionably, the murder of Sir Edmondbury Godfrey, which has my entire approbation. At the same time, it must be observed, that the quantity of murder was not great in this century, at least amongst our own artists; which, perhaps, is attributable to the want of enlightened patronage. *Sint Mœcenates, non deerunt, Flacce, Marones.* Consulting Grant's 'Observations on the Bills of Mortality,' (4th edition, Oxford, 1665,) I find, that out of 229,250, who died in London during one period of twenty years, in the seventeenth century, not more than eighty-six were murdered; that is, about four three-tenths per annum. A small number this, gentlemen, to found an academy upon; and certainly, where the quantity is so small, we have a right to expect that the quality should be first-rate. Perhaps it was; yet, still I am of opinion that the best artist in this century was not equal to the best in that which followed. For instance, however praise-worthy the case of Sir Edmondbury Godfrey may be (and nobody can be more sensible of its merits than I am), still, I cannot consent to place it on a level with that of Mrs. Ruscombe of Bristol, either as to originality of design, or boldness and breadth of style. This good lady's murder took place early in the reign of George III., a reign which was notoriously favorable to the arts generally. She lived in College Green, with a single maid-servant, neither of them having any pretension to the notice of history but what they derived from the great artist whose workmanship I am recording. One fine morning, when all Bristol was alive and in motion, some suspicion arising, the neighbors forced an entrance into the house, and found Mrs. Ruscombe murdered in her bed-room, and the servant murdered on the stairs: this was at noon; and, not more than two hours before, both mistress and servant had been seen alive. To the best of my remembrance, this was in 1764; upwards of sixty years, therefore, have now elapsed, and yet the artist is still undiscovered. The suspicions of posterity have settled upon two pretenders —a baker and a chimney-sweeper. But posterity is wrong; no unpractised artist could have conceived so bold an idea as that of a noon-day murder in the heart of a great city. It was no obscure baker, gentlemen, or anonymous chimney-sweeper, be assured, that executed this work. I know who it was. (*Here there was a general buzz, which at length broke out into open applause; upon which the lecturer blushed, and went on with much earnestness.*) For Heaven's sake, gentlemen, do not mistake me; it was not I that did it. I have not the vanity to think myself equal to any such achievement; be assured that you greatly overrate my poor talents; Mrs. Ruscombe's affair was far beyond my slender abilities. But I came to know who the artist was, from a celebrated surgeon, who assisted at his dissection. This gentleman had a private museum in the way of his profession, one corner of which was occupied by a cast from a man of remarkably fine proportions.

'That,' said the surgeon, 'is a cast from the celebrated Lancashire highwayman, who concealed his profession for some time from his neighbors, by drawing woollen stockings over his horse's legs, and in that way muffling the clatter which he must else have made in riding up a flagged alley that led to his stable. At the time of his execution for highway robbery, I was studying under Cruickshank: and the man's figure was so uncommonly fine, that no money or exertion was spared to get into possession of him with the least possible delay. By the connivance of the under-sheriff he was cut down within the legal time, and instantly put into a chaise and four; so that, when he reached Cruickshank's he was positively not dead. Mr. ——, a young student at that time, had the honor of giving him the *coup de grace*, and finishing the sentence of the law.' This remarkable anecdote, which seemed to imply that all the gentlemen in the dissecting-room were amateurs of our class, struck me a good deal; and I was repeating it one day to a Lancashire lady, who thereupon informed me, that she had herself lived in the neighborhood of that highwayman, and well remembered two circumstances, which combined, in the opinion of all his neighbors, to fix upon him the credit of Mrs. Ruscombe's affair. One was, the fact of his absence for a whole fortnight at the period of that murder: the other, that, within a very little time after, the neighborhood of this highwayman was deluged with dollars: now Mrs. Ruscombe was known to have hoarded about two thousand of that coin. Be the artist, however, who he might, the affair remains a durable monument of his genius; for such was the impression of awe, and the sense of power left behind, by the strength of conception manifested in this murder, that no tenant (as I was told in 1810) had been found up to that time for Mrs. Ruscombe's house.

But, whilst I thus eulogize the Ruscombian case, let me not be supposed to overlook the many other specimens of extraordinary merit spread over the face of this century. Such cases, indeed, as that of Miss Bland, or of Captain Donnellan, and Sir Theophilus Boughton, shall never have any countenance from me. Fie on these dealers in poison, say I: can they not keep to the old honest way of cutting throats, without introducing such abominable innovations from Italy? I consider all these poisoning cases, compared with the legitimate style, as no better than wax-work by the side of sculpture, or a lithographic print by the side of a fine Volpato. But, dismissing these, there remain many excellent works of art in a pure style, such as nobody need be ashamed to own, as every candid connoisseur will admit. *Candid*, observe, I say ; for great allowances must be made in these cases ; no artist can ever be sure of carrying through his own fine preconception. Awkward disturbances will arise ; people will not submit to have their throats cut quietly ; they will run, they will kick, they will bite ; and whilst the portrait painter often has to complain of too much torpor in his subject, the artist, in our line, is generally embarrassed by too much animation. At the same time, however disagreeable to the artist, this tendency in murder to excite and irritate the subject, is certainly one of its advantages to the world in general, which we ought not to overlook, since it favors the development of latent talent. Jeremy Taylor notices with admiration, the extraordinary leaps which people will take under the influence of fear. There was a striking instance of this in the recent case of the M'Keands ; the boy cleared a height, such as he will never clear again to his dying day. Talents also of the most brilliant description for thumping, and indeed for all the gymnastic exercises, have sometimes been developed by the panic which accompanies our artists ; talents else buried and hid under a bushel to the possessors, as much as to their friends. I remember an interesting illustration of this fact, in a case which I learned in Germany.

Riding one day in the neighborhood of Munich, I

overtook a distinguished amateur of our society, whose name I shall conceal. This gentleman informed me that, finding himself wearied with the frigid pleasures (so he called them) of mere amateurship, he had quitted England for the continent — meaning to practise a little professionally. For this purpose he resorted to Germany, conceiving the police in that part of Europe to be more heavy and drowsy than elsewhere. His *debut*, as a practitioner, took place at Mannheim; and, knowing me to be a brother amateur, he freely communicated the whole of his maiden adventure. 'Opposite to my lodging,' said he, 'lived a baker: he was somewhat of a miser, and lived quite alone. Whether it were his great expanse of chalky face, or what else, I know not — but the fact was, I "fancied" him, and resolved to commence business upon his throat, which, by the way, he always carried bare — a fashion which is very irritating to my desires. Precisely at eight o'clock in the evening, I observed that he regularly shut up his windows. One night I watched him when thus engaged — bolted in after him — locked the door — and, addressing him with great suavity, acquainted him with the nature of my errand; at the same time advising him to make no resistance, which would be mutually unpleasant. So saying, I drew out my tools; and was proceeding to operate. But at this spectacle, the baker, who seemed to have been struck by catalepsy at my first announce, awoke into tremendous agitation. "I will *not* be murdered!" he shrieked aloud; "what for will I lose my precious throat?" "What for?" said I; "if for no other reason, for this — that you put alum into your bread. But no matter, alum or no alum, (for I was resolved to forestall any argument on that point,) know that I am a virtuoso in the art of murder — am desirous of improving myself in its details — and am enamored of your vast surface of throat, to which I am determined to be a customer." "Is it so?" said he, "but I'll find you a customer in another line;" and so saying, he threw himself into a boxing attitude. The very idea of his boxing struck me as ludicrous. It is true, a London baker had distinguished himself in the ring, and became known to fame under the title of the Master of the Rolls; but he was young and unspoiled: whereas, this man was a monstrous feather-bed in person, fifty years old, and totally out of condition. Spite of all this, however, and contending against me, who am a master in the art, he made so desperate a defence, that many times I feared he might turn the tables upon me; and that I, an amateur, might be murdered by a rascally baker. What a situation! Minds of sensibility will sympathize with my anxiety. How severe it was, you may understand, by this, that for the first thirteen rounds the baker had the advantage. Round the fourteenth, I received a blow on the right eye, which closed it up; in the end, I believe, this was my salvation; for the anger it roused in me was so great, that, in this, and every one of the three following rounds I floored the baker.

'Round 18th. The baker came up piping, and manifestly the worse for wear. His geometrical exploits in the four last rounds had done him no good. However, he showed some skill in stopping a message which I was sending to his cadaverous mug; in delivering which, my foot slipped, and I went down.

'Round 19th. Surveying the baker, I became ashamed of having been so much bothered by a shapeless mass of dough; and I went in fiercely, and administered some severe punishment. A rally took place — both went down — baker undermost — ten to three on amateur.

'Round 20th. The baker jumped up with surprising agility; indeed, he managed his pins capitally, and fought wonderfully, considering that he was drenched in perspiration; but the shine was now taken out of him, and his game was the mere effect of panic. It was now clear that he could not last much longer. In the course of this round we tried the weaving system, in which I had greatly the advantage, and hit him repeatedly on the conk. My reason for this was, that his conk was covered with carbuncles; and I thought I should vex him by taking such liberties with his conk, which in fact I did.

'The three next rounds, the master of the rolls staggered about like a cow on the ice. Seeing how matters stood, in round twenty-fourth I whispered something into his ear, which sent him down like a shot. It was nothing more than my private opinion of the value of his throat at an annuity office. This little confidential whisper affected him greatly; the very perspiration was frozen on his face, and for the next two rounds I had it all my own way. And when I called *time* for the twenty-seventh round, he lay like a log on the floor.'

After which, said I to the amateur, 'It may be presumed that you accomplished your purpose.' 'You are right,' said he mildly, 'I did; and a great satisfaction, you know, it was to my mind, for by this means I killed two birds with one stone;' meaning that he had both thumped the baker and murdered him. Now, for the life of me, I could not see *that;* for, on the contrary, to my mind it appeared that he had taken two stones to kill one bird, having been obliged to take the conceit out of him first with his fist, and then with his tools. But no matter for his logic. The moral of his story was good, for it showed what an astonishing stimulus to latent talent is contained in any reasonable prospect of being murdered. A pursy, unwieldy, half cataleptic baker of Mannheim had absolutely fought six-and-twenty rounds with an accomplished English boxer merely upon this inspiration; so greatly was natural genius exalted and sublimed by the genial presence of his murderer.

Really, gentlemen, when one hears of such things as these, it becomes a duty, perhaps, a little to soften that extreme asperity with which most men speak of murder. To hear people talk, you would suppose that all the disadvantages and inconveniences were on the side of being murdered, and that there were none at all in *not* being murdered. But considerate men think otherwise. 'Certainly,' says Jeremy Taylor, 'It is a less temporal evil to fall by the rudeness of a sword than the violence of a fever: and the axe' (to which he might have added the ship-carpenter's mallet and the crow-bar) 'a much less affliction than a strangury.' Very true; the bishop talks like a wise man and an amateur, as he [illegible]; and another great philosopher, Marcus Aurelius, was equally above the vulgar prejudices on this subject. He declares it to be one of 'the noblest functions of reason to know whether it is time to walk out of the world or not.' (Book III., Collers' Translation.) No sort of knowledge being rarer than this, surely *that* man must be a most philanthropic character, who undertakes to instruct people in this branch of knowledge gratis, and at no little hazard to himself. All this, however, I throw out only in the way of speculation to future moralists; declaring in the meantime my own private conviction, that very few men commit murder upon philanthropic or patriotic principles, and repeating what I have already said once at least — that, as to the majority of murderers, they are very incorrect characters.

With respect to Williams's murders, the sublimest and most entire in their excellence that ever were committed, I shall not allow myself to speak incidentally. Nothing less than an entire lecture, or even an entire course of lectures, would suffice to expound their merits. But one curious fact, connected with his case, I shall mention, because it seems to imply that the blaze of his genius absolutely dazzled the eye of criminal justice. You all remember, I doubt not, that the instruments with which he executed his first great work, (the murder of the Marrs,) were a ship-carpenter's mallet and a knife. Now the mallet belonged to an old Swede, one John Peterson, and bore his initials. This instrument Williams left behind him, in Marr's house, and it fell into the hands of the magistrates. Now, gentlemen, it is a fact that the publication of this circumstance of the initials led immediately to the apprehension of Williams, and, if made earlier, would have prevented his second great work, (the murder of the Williamsons,) which took place precisely twelve days after. But the magistrates kept back this fact from the public for the entire twelve days, and until that second work was accomplished. That finished, they published it, apparently feeling that Williams had now done enough for his fame, and that his glory was at length placed beyond the reach of accident.

As to Mr. Thurtell's case, I know not what to say. Naturally, I have every disposition to think highly of my predecessor in the chair of this society; and I acknowledge that his lectures were unexceptionable. But speaking ingenuously, I do really think that his principal performance, as an artist, has been much overrated. I admit that at first I was myself carried away by the general enthusiasm. On the morning when the murder was made known in London, there was the fullest meeting of amateurs that I have ever known since the days of Williams; old bed-ridden connoisseurs, who had got into a peevish way of sneering and complaining 'that there was nothing doing,' now hobbled down to our club-room: such hilarity, such benign expression of general satisfaction, I have rarely witnessed. On every side you saw people shaking hands, congratulating each other, and forming dinner parties for the evening; and nothing was to be heard but triumphant challenges of—'Well! will *this* do?' 'Is *this* the right thing?' 'Are you satisfied at last?' But, in the midst of this, I remember we all grew silent on hearing the old cynical amateur, L. S——, that *laudator temporis acti*, stumping along with his wooden leg; he entered the room with his usual scowl, and, as he advanced, he continued to growl and stutter the whole way — 'Not an original idea in the whole piece — mere plagiarism, — base plagiarism from hints that I threw out! Besides, his style is as hard as Albert Durer, and as coarse as Fuseli.' Many thought that this was mere jealousy, and general waspishness; but I confess that, when the first glow of enthusiasm had subsided, I have found most judicious critics to agree that there was something *falsetto* in the style of Thurtell. The fact is, he was a member of our society, which naturally gave a friendly bias to our judgments; and his person was universally familiar to the cockneys, which gave him, with the whole London public, a temporary popularity, that his pretensions are not capable of supporting; for *opinionum commenta delet dies, naturæ judicia confirmat.* There was, however, an unfinished design of Thurtell's for the murder of a man with a pair of dumb-bells, which I admired greatly; it was a mere outline, that he never completed; but to my mind it seemed every way superior to his chief work. I remember that there was great regret expressed by some amateurs that this sketch should have been left in an unfinished state: but there I cannot agree with them; for the fragments and first bold outlines of original artists have often a felicity about them which is apt to vanish in the management of the details.

The case of the M'Keands I consider far beyond the vaunted performance of Thurtell, — indeed above all praise; and bearing that relation, in fact, to the immortal works of Williams, which the Æneid bears to the Iliad.

But it is now time that I should say a few words about the principles of murder, not with a view to regulate your practice, but your judgment: as to old women, and the mob of newspaper readers, they are pleased with anything, provided it is bloody enough. But the mind of sensibility requires something more. *First*, then, let us speak of the kind of person who is adapted to the purpose of the murderer; *secondly*, of the place where; *thirdly*, of the time when, and other little circumstances.

As to the person, I suppose it is evident that he ought to be a good man; because, if he were not, he might himself, by possibility, be contemplating murder at the very time; and such 'diamond-cut-diamond' tussles, though pleasant enough where nothing better is stirring, are really not what a critic can allow himself to call murders. I could mention some people (I name no names) who have been murdered by other people in a dark lane; and so far all seemed correct enough; but, on looking farther into the matter, the public have become aware that the murdered party was himself, at the moment, planning to rob his murderer, at the least, and possibly to murder him, if he had been strong enough. Whenever that is the case, or may be thought to be the case, farewell to all the genuine effects of the art. For the final purpose of murder, considered as a fine art, is precisely the same as that of tragedy, in Aristotle's account of it, viz., 'to cleanse the heart by means of pity and terror.' Now, terror there may be, but how can there be any pity for one tiger destroyed by another tiger?

It is also evident that the person selected ought not

to be a public character. For instance, no judicious artist would have attempted to murder Abraham Newland. For the case was this: everybody read so much about Abraham Newland, and so few people ever saw him, that there was a fixed belief that he was an abstract idea. And I remember that once, when I happened to mention that I had dined at a coffee-house in company with Abraham Newland, everybody looked scornfully at me, as though I had pretended to have played at billiards with Prester John, or to have had an affair of honor with the Pope. And, by the way, the Pope would be a very improper person to murder: for he has such a virtual ubiquity as the father of Christendom, and, like the cuckoo, is so often heard but never seen, that I suspect most people regard *him* also as an abstract idea. Where, indeed, a public character is in the habit of giving dinners, 'with every delicacy of the season,' the case is very different: every person is satisfied that *he* is no abstract idea; and, therefore, there can be no impropriety in murdering him; only that his murder will fall into the class of assassinations, which I have not yet treated.

Thirdly. The subject chosen ought to be in good health: for it is absolutely barbarous to murder a sick person, who is usually quite unable to bear it. On this principle, no cockney ought to be chosen who is above twenty-five, for after that age he is sure to be dyspeptic. Or at least, if a man will hunt in that warren, he ought to murder a couple at one time; if the cockneys chosen should be tailors, he will of course think it his duty, on the old established equation, to murder eighteen. And, here, in this attention to the comfort of sick people, you will observe the usual effect of a fine art to soften and refine the feelings. The world in general, gentlemen, are very bloody-minded; and all they want in a murder is a copious effusion of blood; gaudy display in this point is enough for *them*. But the enlightened connoisseur is more refined in his taste; and from our art, as from all the other liberal arts when thoroughly cultivated, the result is — to improve and to humanize the heart; so true is it, that —

——'Ingenuas didicisse fideliter artes,
Emollit mores, nec sinit esse feros.'

A philosophic friend, well known for his philanthropy and general benignity, suggests that the subject chosen ought also to have a family of young children wholly dependent on his exertions, by way of deepening the pathos. And, undoubedly, this is a judicious caution. Yet I would not insist too keenly on this condition. Severe good taste unquestionably demands it; but still, where the man was otherwise unobjectionable in point of morals and health, I would not look with too curious a jealousy to a restriction which might have the effect of narrowing the artist's sphere.

So much for the person. As to the time, the place, and the tools, I have many things to say, which at present I have no room for. The good sense of the practitioner has usually directed him to night and privacy. Yet there have not been wanting cases where this rule was departed from with excellent effect. In respect to time, Mrs. Ruscombe's case is a beautiful exception, which I have already noticed;

and in respect both to time and place, there is a fine exception in the annals of Edinburgh, (year 1805,) familiar to every child in Edinburgh, but which has unaccountably been defrauded of its due portion of fame amongst English amateurs. The case I mean is that of a porter to one of the banks, who was murdered whilst carrying a bag of money, in broad daylight, on turning out of the High Street, one of the most public streets in Europe, and the murderer is to this hour undiscovered.

> 'Sed fugit interea, fugit irreparabile tempus,
> Singula dum capti circumvectamur amore.'

And now, gentlemen, in conclusion, let me again solemnly disclaim all pretensions on my own part to the character of a professional man. I never attempted any murder in my life, except in the year 1801, upon the body of a tom-cat; and *that* turned out differently from my intention. My purpose, I own, was downright murder. 'Semper ego auditor tantum?' said I, 'nunquamne reponam?' And I went down stairs in search of Tom at one o'clock on a dark night, with the 'animus,' and no doubt with the fiendish looks, of a murderer. But when I found him, he was in the act of plundering the pantry of bread and other things. Now this gave a new turn to the affair; for the time being one of general scarcity, when even Christians were reduced to the use of potato-bread, rice-bread, and all sorts of things, it was downright treason in a tom-cat to be wasting good wheaten-bread in the way he was doing. It instantly became a patriotic duty to put him to death; and as I raised aloft and shook the glittering steel, I fancied myself rising like Brutus, effulgent from a crowd of patriots, and, as I stabbed him, I

> 'called aloud on Tully's name,
> And bade the father of his country hail!'

Since then, what wandering thoughts I may have had of attempting the life of an ancient ewe, of a superannuated hen, and such 'small deer,' are locked up in the secrets of my own breast; but for the higher departments of the art, I confess myself to be utterly unfit. My ambition does not rise so high. No, gentlemen, in the words of Horace,

> '——— fungar vice cotis, acutum
> Reddere quæ ferrum valet, exsors ipsa secandi.'

SECOND PAPER ON MURDER,

CONSIDERED AS ONE OF THE FINE ARTS.

DOCTOR NORTH: You are a liberal man: liberal in the true classical sense, not in the slang sense of modern politicians and education-mongers. Being so, I am sure that you will sympathize with my case. I am an ill-used man, Dr. North — particularly ill used; and, with your permission, I will briefly explain how. A black scene of calumny will be laid open; but you, Doctor, will make all things square again. One frown from you, directed to the proper quarter, or a warning shake of the crutch, will set me right in public opinion, which at present, I am sorry to say, is rather hostile to me and mine — all owing to the wicked arts of slanderers. But you shall hear.

A good many years ago you may remember that I came forward in the character of a *dilettante* in murder. Perhaps *dilettante* may be too strong a word. *Connoisseur* is better suited to the scruples and infirmity of public taste. I suppose there is no harm in *that* at least. A man is not bound to put his eyes, ears, and understanding into his breeches pocket when he meets with a murder. If he is not in a downright comatose state, I suppose he must see that one murder is better or worse than another in point of good taste. Murders have their little differences and shades of merit as well as statues, pictures, oratorios, cameos, intaglios, or what not. You may be angry with the man for talking too much, or too publicly, (as to the too much, that I deny — a man can never cultivate his taste too highly ;) but you must allow him to think, at any rate ; and you, Doctor, you think, I am sure, both deeply and correctly on the subject. Well, would you believe it? all my neighbors came to hear of that little æsthetic essay which you had published ; and, unfortunately, hearing at the very same time of a club that I was connected with, and a dinner at which I presided — both tending to the same little object as the essay, viz., the diffusion of a just taste among her majesty's subjects, they got up the most barbarous calumnies against me. In particular, they said that I, or that the club, which comes to the same thing, had offered bounties on well conducted homicides — with a scale of drawbacks, in case of any one defect or flaw, according to a table issued to private friends. Now, Doctor, I'll tell you the whole truth about the dinner and the club, and you'll see how malicious the world is. But first let me tell you, confidentially, what my real principles are upon the matters in question.

As to murder, I never committed one in my life. It's a well known thing amongst all my friends. I can get a paper to certify as much, signed by lots of people. Indeed, if you come to that, I doubt whether many people could produce as strong a certificate. Mine would be as big as a table-cloth. There is indeed one member of the club, who pretends to say that he caught me once making too free with his throat on a club night, after every body else had retired. But, observe, he shuffles in his story according to his state of civilation. When not far gone, he contents himself with saying that he caught me ogling his throat; and that I was melancholy for some weeks after, and that my voice sounded in a way expressing, to the nice ear of a connoisseur, *the sense of opportunities lost* — but the club all know that he's a disappointed man himself, and that he speaks querulously at times about the fatal neglect of a man's coming abroad without his tools. Besides, all this is an affair between two amateurs, and every body makes allowances for little asperities and sorenesses in such a case. 'But,' say you, 'if no murderer, my correspondent may have encouraged, or even have bespoken a murder.' No, upon my honor — nothing of the kind. And that was the very point I wished to argue for your satisfaction. The truth is, I am a very particular man in everything relating to murder; and perhaps I carry my delicacy too far. The Stagyrite most justly, and possibly with a view to my case, placed virtue in the τὸ μέσον or middle point between two extremes. A golden mean is certainly what every man should aim at. But it is easier talking than doing; and, my infirmity being notoriously too much milkiness of heart, I find it difficult to maintain that steady equatorial line between the two poles of too much murder on the one hand, and too little on the other. I am too soft — Doctor, too soft; and people get excused through me — nay, go through life without an attempt made upon them, that ought not to be excused. I believe if I had the management of things, there would hardly be a murder from year's end to year's end. In fact I'm for virtue, and goodness, and all that sort of thing. And two instances I'll give you to what an extremity I carry my virtue. The first may seem a trifle; but not if you knew my nephew, who was certainly born to be hanged, and would have been so long ago, but for my restraining voice. He is horribly ambitious, and thinks himself a man of cultivated taste in most branches of murder, whereas, in fact, he has not one idea on the subject, but such as he has stolen from me. This is so well known, that the club has twice blackballed him, though every indulgence was shown to him as my relative. People came to me and said — 'Now really, President, we would do much to serve a relative of yours. But still, what can be said? You know yourself that he'll disgrace us. If we were to elect him, why, the next thing we should hear of would be some vile butcherly murder, by way of justifying our choice. And what sort of a concern would it be? You know, as well as we do, that it would be a disgraceful affair, more worthy of the shambles than of an artist's *attelier*. He would fall upon some great big man, some huge farmer returning drunk from a fair. There would be plenty of blood, and *that* he would expect us to take in lieu of taste, finish, scenical grouping. Then, again, how would he tool? Why, most probably with a cleaver and a couple of paving stones: so that the whole *coup d'œil* would remind you rather of some hideous ogre or cyclops, than of the delicate operator of the nineteenth century.' The picture was drawn with the hand of truth; *that* I could not but allow, and, as to personal feelings in the matter, I dismissed them from the first. The next morning I spoke to my nephew — I was delicately situated, as you see, but I determined that no consideration should induce me to flinch from my duty. 'John,' said I, 'you seem to me to have taken an erroneous view of life and its duties. Pushed on by ambition, you are dreaming rather of what it might be glorious to attempt, than what it would be possible for you to accomplish. Believe me, it is not necessary to a man's respectability that he should commit a murder. Many a man has passed through life most respectably, without attempting any species of homicide — good, bad, or indifferent. It is your first duty to ask yourself, *quid valeant humeri, quid ferre recusent?* we cannot all be brilliant men in this life. And it is for your interest to be contented rather with a humble station well filled, than to shock every body with failures, the more conspicuous by contrast with the ostentation of their promises.' John made no answer, he looked very sulky at the moment, and I am in high hopes that I have saved a near relation from making a fool of himself by attempting what is as much beyond his capacity as an epic poem. Others, however, tell me that he is meditating a revenge upon me and the whole club. But let this be as it may, *liberavi animam meam;* and, as you see, have run some risk with a wish to diminish the amount of homicide. But the other case still more forcibly illustrates my virtue. A man came to me as a candidate for the place of my servant, just then vacant. He had the reputation of having dabbled a little in our art; some said not without merit. What startled me, however, was, that he supposed this art to be part of his regular duties in my service. Now that was a thing I would not allow; so I said at once, 'Richard (or James, as the case might be,) you misunderstand my character. If a man will and must practise this difficult (and allow me to add, dangerous) branch of art — if he has an overruling genius for it, why, he might as well pursue his studies whilst living in my service as in another's. And also, I may observe, that it can do no harm either to himself or to the subject on whom he operates, that he should be guided by men of more taste than himself. Genius may do much, but long study of the art must always entitle a man to offer advice. So far I will go — general principles I will suggest. But as to any particular case, once for all I will have nothing to do with it. Never tell me of any special work of art you are meditating — I set my face against it *in toto*. For if once a man indulges himself in murder, very soon he comes to think little of robbing; and from robbing he comes next to drinking and Sabbath-breaking, and from that to incivility and procrastination. Once begin upon this downward path, you never know where you are to stop. Many a man has dated his ruin from some murder or other that perhaps he thought little of at the time. *Principiis obsta* — that's my rule.' Such was my speech, and I have always acted up to it; so if that is not being virtuous, I should be glad to know what is. But now about the dinner and the club. The club was not particularly of my creation; it arose pretty much as other similar associations, for the propagation of truth and the communication of new ideas, rather from the necessities of things than upon any one man's suggestion. As to the dinner, if any man more than another could be held responsible for that, it was a member known amongst us by the name of *Toad-in-the-hole.* He was so called from his gloomy misanthropical disposition, which led him into constant disparagements of all modern murders as vicious abortions, belonging to no authentic school of art. The finest performances of our own age, he snarled at cynically; and at length this querulous humor grew upon him so much, and he became so notorious as a *laudator temporis acti*, that few people cared to seek his society. This made him still more fierce and truculent. He went about muttering and growling; wherever you met him he was soliloquizing and saying, 'despicable pretender — without grouping — without two ideas upon handling — without' — and there you lost him. At length existence seemed to be painful to him; he rarely spoke, he seemed conversing with phantoms in the air, his housekeeper informed us that his reading was nearly confined to *God's Revenge upon Murder*, by Reynolds, and a more ancient book of the same title, noticed by Sir Walter Scott, in his *Fortunes of Nigel.* Sometimes, perhaps, he might read in the Newgate Calendar down to the year 1788, but he never looked into a book more recent. In fact, he had a theory with regard to the French Revolution, as having been the great cause of degeneration in murder. 'Very soon, sir,' he used to say, 'men will have lost the art of killing poultry: the very rudiments of the art will have perished!' In the year 1811, he retired from general society. Toad-in-the-hole was no more seen in any public resort.

We missed him from his wonted haunts — nor up the lawn, nor at the wood was he. By the side of the main conduit his listless length at noontide he would stretch, and pore upon the filth that muddled by. 'Even dogs are not what they were, sir — not what they should be. I remember in my grandfather's time that some dogs had an idea of murder. I have known a mastiff lie in ambush for a rival, sir, and murder him with pleasing circumstances of good taste. Yes, sir, I knew a tom-cat that was an assassin. But now' —— and then, the subject growing too painful, he dashed his hand to his forehead, and went off abruptly in a homeward direction towards his favorite conduit, where he was seen by an amateur in such a state that he thought it dangerous to address him. Soon after he shut himself entirely up; it was understood that he had resigned himself to melancholy; and at length the prevailing notion was, that Toad-in-the-hole had hanged himself.

The world was wrong *there*, as it had been on some other questions. Toad-in-the-hole might be sleeping, but dead he was not; and of that we soon had ocular proof. One morning in 1812, an amateur surprised us with the news that he had seen Toad-in-the-hole brushing with hasty steps the dews away to meet the postman by the conduit side. Even that was something: how much more, to hear that he had shaved his beard — had laid aside his sad-colored clothes, and was adorned like a bridegroom of ancient days. What could be the meaning of all this? Was Toad-in-the-hole mad? or how? Soon after the secret was explained — in more than a figurative sense 'the murder was out.' For in came the London morning papers, by which it appeared that but three days before a murder, the most superb of the century by many degrees, had occurred in the heart of London. I need hardly say, that this was the great exterminating *chef-d'œuvre* of Williams at Mr. Marr's, No. 29, Ratcliffe Highway. That was the *début* of the artist; at least for anything the public knew. What occurred at Mr. Williamson's twelve nights afterwards — the second work turned out from the same chisel — some people pronounced even superior. But Toad-in-the-hole always 'reclaimed' — he was even angry at comparisons. 'This vulgar *gout de comparaison*, as La Bruyère calls it,' he would often remark, 'will be our ruin; each work has its own separate characteristics — each in and for itself is incomparable. One, perhaps, might suggest the *Iliad* — the other the *Odyssey*: what do you get by such comparisons? Neither ever was, or will be surpassed; and when you 've talked for hours, you must still come back to that.' Vain, however, as all criticism might be, he often said that volumes might be written on each case for itself; and he even proposed to publish in quarto on the subject.

Meantime, how had Toad-in-the-hole happened to hear of this great work of art so early in the morning? He had received an account by express, dispatched by a correspondent in London, who watched the progress of art on *Toady's* behalf, with a general commission to send off a special express, at whatever cost, in the event of any estimable works appearing — how much more upon occasion of a *ne plus ultra* in art! The express arrived in the night-time; Toad-in-the-hole was then gone to bed; he had been muttering and grumbling for hours, but of course he was called up. On reading the account, he threw his arms round the express, called him his brother and his preserver; settled a pension upon him for three lives, and expressed his regret at not having it in his power to knight him. We, on our part — we amateurs, I mean — having heard that he was abroad, and therefore had *not* hanged himself, made sure of soon seeing him amongst us. Accordingly he soon arrived, knocked over the porter on his road to the reading-room; he seized every man's hand as he passed him — wrung it almost frantically, and kept ejaculating, 'Why, now here's something like a murder! — this is the real thing — this is genuine — this is what you can approve, can recommend to a friend: this — says every man, on reflection — this is the thing that ought to be!' Then, looking at particular friends, he said — 'Why, Jack, how are you? Why, Tom, how are you? Bless me, you look ten years younger than when I last saw you.' 'No, sir,' I replied, 'It is you who look ten years younger.' 'Do I? well, I should 'nt wonder if I did; such works are enough to make us all young.' And in fact the general opinion is, that Toad-in-the-hole would have died but for this regeneration of art, which he called a second age of Leo the Tenth; and it was our duty, he said solemnly, to commemorate it. At present, and *en attendant* — rather as an occasion for a public participation in public sympathy, than as in itself any commensurate testimony of our interest — he proposed that the club should meet and dine together. A splendid public dinner, therefore, was given by the club; to which all amateurs were invited from a distance of one hundred miles.

Of this dinner, there are ample short-hand notes amongst the archives of the club. But they are not 'extended,' to speak diplomatically; and the reporter is missing — I believe, murdered. Meantime, in years long after that day, and on an occasion perhaps equally interesting, viz., the turning up of Thugs and Thuggism, another dinner was given. Of this I myself kept notes, for fear of another accident to the short-hand reporter. And I here subjoin them. Toad-in-the-hole, I must mention, was present at this dinner. In fact, it was one of its sentimental incidents. Being as old as the valleys at the dinner of 1812, naturally he was as old as the hills at the Thug dinner of 1838. He had taken to wearing his beard again; why, or with what view, it passes my persimmon to tell you. But so it was. And his appearance was most benign and venerable. Nothing could equal the angelic radiance of his smile as he inquired after the unfortunate reporter, (whom, as a piece of private scandal, I should tell you that he was himself supposed to have murdered, in a rapture of creative art:) the answer was, with roars of laughter, from the under-sheriff of our county — 'Non est inventus.' Toad-in-the-hole laughed outrageously at this: in fact, we all thought he was choking; and, at the earnest request of the company, a musical composer furnished a most beautiful glee upon the occasion, which was sung five times after dinner, with universal applause and inextinguishable laughter, the words being these, (and the chorus so contrived, as most beautifully to mimic the peculiar laughter of Toad-in-the-hole:) —

'Et interrogatum est à Toad-in-the-hole — Ubi est ille reporter?
Et responsum est cum cachinno — Non est inventus.

CHORUS.

'Deinde iteratum est ab omnibus, cum cachinnatione undulante — Non est inventus.'

Toad-in-the-hole, I ought to mention, about nine years before, when an express from Edinburgh brought him the earliest intelligence of the Burke-and-Hare revolution in the art, went mad upon the spot; and, instead of a pension to the express for even one life, or a knighthood, endeavored to Burke him; in consequence of which he was put into a strait waistcoat. And that was the reason we had no dinner then. But now all of us were alive and kicking, strait-waistcoaters and others; in fact, not one absentee was reported upon the entire roll. There were also many foreign amateurs present.

Dinner being over, and the cloth drawn, there was a general call made for the new glee of *Non est inventus;* but, as this would have interfered with the requisite gravity of the company during the earlier toasts, I overruled the call. After the national toasts had been given, the first official toast of the day was, *The Old Man of the Mountains* — drunk in solemn silence.

Toad-in-the-hole returned thanks in a neat speech. He likened himself to the Old Man of the Mountains, in a few brief allusions, that made the company absolutely yell with laughter; and he concluded with giving the health of

Mr. Von Hammer, with many thanks to him for his learned History of the Old Man and his subjects the assassins.

Upon this I rose and said, that doubtless most of the company were aware of the distinguished place assigned by orientalists to the very learned Turkish scholar Von Hammer the Austrian; that he had made the profoundest researches into our art as connected with those early and eminent artists the Syrian assassins in the period of the Crusaders; that his work had been for several years deposited, as a rare treasure of art, in the library of the club. Even the author's name, gentlemen, pointed him out as the historian of our art — Von Hammer ——

'Yes, yes,' interrupted Toad-in-the-hole, who never can sit still — 'Yes, yes, Von Hammer — he's the man for a *malleus hæreticorum:* think rightly of our art, or he's the man to tickle your catastrophes. You all know what consideration Williams bestowed on the hammer, or the ship carpenter's mallet, which is the same thing. Gentlemen, I give you another great hammer — Charles the Hammer, the Marteau, or, in old French, the Martel — he hammered the Saracens till they were all as dead as door-nails — he did, believe me.'

'*Charles Martel*, with all the honors.'

But the explosion of Toad-in-the-hole, together with the uproarious cheers for the grandpapa of Charlemagne, had now made the company unmanageable. The orchestra was again challenged with shouts the stormiest for the new glee. I made again a powerful effort to overrule the challenge. I might as well have talked to the winds. I foresaw a tempestuous evening; and I ordered myself to be strengthened with three waiters on each side; the vice-president with as many. Symptoms of unruly enthusiasm were beginning to show out; and I own that I myself was considerably excited as the orchestra opened with its storm of music, and the impassioned glee began — '*Et interrogatum est à Toad-in-the-hole — Ubi est ille Reporter?*' And the frenzy of the passion became absolutely convulsing, as the full chorus fell in — '*Et iteratum est ab omnibus — Non est inventus.*'

By this time I saw how things were going: wine and music were making most of the amateurs wild. Particularly Toad-in-the-hole, though considerably above a hundred years old, was getting as vicious as a young leopard. It was a fixed impression with the company that he had murdered the reporter in the year 1812; since which time (viz. twenty-six years) 'ille reporter' had been constantly reported 'Non est inventus.' Consequently, the glee about himself, which of itself was most tumultuous and jubilant, carried him off his feet. Like the famous choral songs amongst the citizens of Abdera, nobody could hear it without a contagious desire for falling back into the agitating music of 'Et interrogatum est à Toad-in-the-hole,' &c. I enjoined vigilance upon my assessors, and the business of the evening proceeded.

The next toast was — *The Jewish Sicarii.*

Upon which I made the following explanation to the company: — 'Gentlemen, I am sure it will interest you all to hear that the assassins, ancient as they were, had a race of predecessors in the very same country. All over Syria, but particularly in Palestine, during the early years of the Emperor Nero, there was a band of murderers, who prosecuted their studies in a very novel manner. They did not practise in the night-time, or in lonely places; but justly considering that great crowds are in themselves a sort of darkness by means of the dense pressure and the impossibility of finding out who it was that gave the blow, they mingled with mobs everywhere; particularly at the great paschal feast in Jerusalem; where they actually had the audacity, as Josephus assures us, to press into the temple. — and whom should they choose for operating upon but Jonathan himself, the Pontifex Maximus? They murdered him, gentlemen, as beautifully as if they had had him alone on a moonless night in a dark lane. And when it was asked, who was the murderer, and where he was' ——

'Why, then, it was answered,' interrupted Toad-in-the-hole, '*Non est inventus.*' And then, in spite of all I could do or say, the orchestra opened, and the whole company began — 'Et interrogatum est à Toad-in-the-hole — Ubi est ille Sicarius? Et responsum est ab omnibus — *Non est inventus.*'

When the tempestuous chorus had subsided, I began again: — 'Gentlemen, you will find a very circumstantial account of the Sicarii in at least three different parts of Josephus; once in Book XX. sect. v. c. 8, of his *Antiquities;* once in Book I. of his *Wars:* but in sect. 10 of the chapter first cited you will find a particular description of their tooling. This is what he says — 'They tooled with small scymetars not much different from the Persian *acinacæ*, but more curved, and for all the world most like the Roman sickles or *sicæ*.' It is perfectly magnificent, gentlemen, to hear the sequel of their history. Perhaps the only case on record where a regular army of murderers was assembled, a *justus exercitus*, was in the case of these *Sicarii*. They mustered in such strength in the wilderness, that Festus himself was obliged to march against them with the Roman legionary force.'

Upon which Toad-in-the-hole, that cursed interrupter, broke out a-singing — 'Et interrogatum est à Toad-in-the-hole — Ubi est ille exercitus? Et responsum est ab omnibus — Non est inventus.'

'No, no, Toad — you are wrong for once: that army *was* found, and was all cut to pieces in the desert. Heavens, gentlemen, what a sublime picture! The Roman legions — the wilderness — Jerusalem in the distance — an army of murderers in the foreground!'

Mr. R., a member, now gave the next toast — 'To the further improvement of Tooling, and thanks to the Committee for their services.'

Mr. L., on behalf of the committee who had reported on that subject, returned thanks. He made an interesting extract from the report, by which it appeared how very much stress had been laid formerly on the mode of tooling, by the fathers, both Greek and Latin. In confirmation of this pleasing fact, he made a very striking statement in reference to the earliest work of antediluvian art. Father Mersenne, that learned Roman Catholic, in page one thousand four hundred and thirty-one[1] of his operose Commentary on Genesis, mentions, on the authority of several rabbis, that the quarrel of Cain with Abel was about a young woman; that, by various accounts, Cain had tooled with his teeth, [Abelem fuisse *morsibus* dilaceratum à Cain;]

[1] 'Page one thousand four hundred and thirty-one' —*literally*, good reader, and no joke at all.

by many others, with the jaw-bone of an ass; which is the tooling adopted by most painters. But it is pleasing to the mind of sensibility to know that, as science expanded, sounder views were adopted. One author contends for a pitchfork, St. Chrysostom for a sword, Irenæus for a scythe, and Prudentius for a hedging-bill. This last writer delivers his opinion thus: —

> 'Frater, probatæ sanctitatis æmulus,
> Germana curvo colla frangit sarculo:'

i. e. his brother, jealous of his attested sanctity, fractures his brotherly throat with a curved hedging-bill. 'All which is respectfully submitted by your committee, not so much as decisive of the question, (for it is not,) but in order to impress upon the youthful mind the importance which has ever been attached to the quality of the tooling by such men as Chrysostom and Irenæus.'

'Dang Irenæus!' said Toad-in-the-hole, who now rose impatiently to give the next toast: — 'Our Irish friends; and a speedy revolution in their mode of tooling, as well as everything else connected with the art!'

'Gentlemen, I'll tell you the plain truth. Every day of the year we take up a paper, we read the opening of a murder. We say, this is good, this is charming, this is excellent! But, behold you! scarcely have we read a little farther, before the word Tipperary or Ballina-something betrays the Irish manufacture. Instantly we loath it; we call to the waiter; we say, "Waiter, take away this paper; send it out of the house; it is absolutely offensive to all just taste." I appeal to every man whether, on finding a murder (otherwise perhaps promising enough) to be Irish, he does not feel himself as much insulted as when Madeira being ordered, he finds it to be Cape; or, when, taking up what he takes to be a mushroom, it turns out what children call a toad-stool. Tithes, politics, or something wrong in principle, vitiate every Irish murder. Gentlemen, this must be reformed, or Ireland will not be a land to live in; at least, if we do live there, we must import all our murders, that's clear.' Toad-in-the-hole sat down growling with suppressed wrath, and the universal 'Hear, hear!' sufficiently showed that he spoke the general feeling.

The next toast was—'The sublime epoch of Burkism and Harism!'

This was drunk with enthusiasm; and one of the members, who spoke to the question, made a very curious communication to the company:—'Gentlemen, we fancy Burkism to be a pure invention of our own times: and in fact no Pancirollus has ever enumerated this branch of art when writing *de rebus deperditis.* Still I have ascertained that the essential principle of the art *was* known to the ancients, although like the art of painting upon glass, of making the myrrhine cups, &c., it was lost in the dark ages for want of encouragement. In the famous collection of Greek epigrams made by Planudes is one upon a very charming little case of Burkism: it is a perfect little gem of art. The epigram itself I cannot lay my hand upon at this moment, but the following is an abstract of it by Salmasius, as I find it in his notes on Vopiscus: "Est et elegans epigramma Lucilii, (well he might call it 'elegans!') ubi medicus et pollinctor de compacto sic egerunt, ut medicus ægros omnes curæ suæ commissos occideret:' this was the basis of the contract, you see, that on the one part the doctor, for himself and his assigns, doth undertake and contract duly and truly to murder all the patients committed to his charge: but why? There lies the beauty of the case —"Et ut pollinctori amico suo traderet pollingendos." The *pollinctor*, you are aware, was a person whose business it was to dress and prepare dead bodies for burial. The original ground of the transaction appears to have been sentimental: "He was my friend," says the murderous doctor; "he was dear to me," in speaking of the pollinctor. But the law, gentlemen, is stern and harsh: the law will not hear of these tender motives: to sustain a contract of this nature in law, it is essential that a "consideration" should be given. Now what *was* the consideration? For thus far all is on the side of the pollinctor: he will be well paid for his services; but, meantime, the generous, the noble-minded doctor gets nothing. What *was* the little consideration again, I ask, which the law would insist on the doctor's taking? You shall hear: "Et ut pollinctor vicissim τελαμῶνας quos furabatur de pollinctione mortuorum medico mitteret doni ad alliganda vulnera eorum quos curabat." Now, the case is clear: the whole went on a principle of reciprocity which would have kept up the trade for ever. The doctor was also a surgeon: he could not murder *all* his patients: some of the surgical patients must be retained intact; *re infectâ*. For these he wanted linen bandages. But, unhappily, the Romans wore woollen, on which account they bathed so often. Meantime, there *was* linen to be had in Rome; but it was monstrously dear; and the τελαμῶνες or linen swathing bandages, in which superstition obliged them to bind up corpses, would answer capitally for the surgeon. The doctor, therefore, contracts to furnish his friend with a constant succession of corpses, provided, and be it understood always, that his said friend in return should supply him with one half of the articles he would receive from the friends of the parties murdered or to be murdered. The doctor invariably recommended his invaluable friend the pollinctor, (whom let us call the undertaker;) the undertaker, with equal regard to the sacred rights of friendship, uniformly recommended the doctor. Like Pylades and Orestes, they were models of a perfect friendship: in their lives they were lovely, and on the gallows, it is to be hoped, they were not divided.

'Gentlemen, it makes me laugh horribly, when I think of those two friends drawing and redrawing on each other: "Pollinctor in account with Doctor, debtor by sixteen corpses: creditor by forty-five bandages, two of which damaged." Their names unfortunately are lost; but I conceive they must have been Quintus Burkius and Publius Harius. By the way, gentlemen, has anybody heard lately of Hare? I understand he is comfortably settled in Ireland, considerably to the west, and does a little business now and then; but, as he observes with a sigh, only as a retailer — nothing like the fine thriving wholesale concern so carelessly blown up at Edinburgh. "You see what comes of neglecting business," — is the chief moral, the ἐπιμύθιον, as Æsop would say, which he draws from his past experience.'

At length came the toast of the day — *Thugdom in all its branches.*

The speeches *attempted* at this crisis of the dinner were past all counting. But the applause was so furious, the music so stormy, and the crashing of glasses so incessant, from the general resolution never again to drink an inferior toast from the same glass, that my power is not equal to the task of reporting. Besides which, Toad-in-the-hole now became quite ungovernable. He kept firing pistols in every direction; sent his servant for a blunderbuss, and talked of loading with ball-cartridge. We conceived that his former madness had returned at the mention of Burke and Hare; or that, being again weary of life, he had resolved to go off in a general massacre. This we could not think of allowing; it became indispensable, therefore, to kick him out, which we did with universal consent, the whole company lending their toes *uno pede*, as I may say, though pitying his gray hairs and his angelic smile. During the operation the orchestra poured in their old chorus. The universal company sang, and (what surprised us most of all) Toad-in-the-hole joined us furiously in singing —

'Et interrogatum est ab omnibus—Ubi est ille Toad-in-the-hole?
Et responsum est ab omnibus — Non est inventus.'

JOAN OF ARC.[1]

IN REFERENCE TO M. MICHELET'S HISTORY OF FRANCE.

WHAT is to be thought of *her?* What is to be thought of the poor shepherd girl from the hills and forests of Lorraine, that — like the Hebrew shepherd boy from the hills and forests of Judæa — rose suddenly out of the quiet, out of the safety, out of the religious inspiration, rooted in deep pastoral solitudes, to a station in the van of armies, and to the more perilous station at the right hand of kings? The Hebrew boy inaugurated his patriotic mission by an *act*, by a victorious *act*, such as no man could deny. But so did the girl of Lorraine, if we read her story as it was read by those who saw her nearest. Adverse armies bore witness to the boy as no pretender; but so they did to the gentle girl. Judged by the voices of all who saw them *from a station of good will*, both were found true and loyal to any promises involved in their first acts. Enemies it was that made the difference between their subsequent fortunes. The boy rose — to a splendor and a noonday prosperity, both personal and public, that rang through the records of his people, and became a bye-word amongst his posterity for a thousand years, until the sceptre was departing from Judah. The poor, forsaken girl, on the contrary, drank not herself from that cup of rest which she had secured for France. She never sang together with the songs that rose in her native Domrémy, as echoes to the departing steps of invaders. She mingled not in the festal dances at Vaucouleurs which celebrated in rapture the redemption of France. No! for her voice was then silent: No! for her feet were dust. Pure, innocent, noble-hearted girl! whom, from earliest youth, ever I believed in as full of truth and self-sacrifice, this was amongst the strongest pledges for *thy* side, that never once — no, not for a moment of weakness — didst thou revel in the vision of coronets and honor from man. Coronets for thee! O no! Honors, if they come when all is over, are for those that share thy blood.[2] Daughter of Domrémy, when the gratitude of thy king shall awaken, thou wilt be sleeping the sleep of the dead. Call her, King of France, but she will not hear thee! Cite her by thy apparitors to come and receive a robe of honor, but she will be found *en contumace*. When the thunders of universal France, as even yet may happen, shall proclaim the grandeur of the poor shepherd girl that gave up all for her country — thy ear, young shepherd girl, will have been deaf for five centuries. To suffer and to do, that was thy portion in this life; to *do* — never for thyself, always for others; to *suffer* — never in the persons of generous champions, always in thy own — that was thy destiny; and not for a moment was it hidden from thyself. Life, thou saidst, is short: and the sleep which is in the grave, is long! Let me use that life, so transitory, for the glory of those heavenly dreams destined to comfort the sleep which is so long. This pure creature — pure from every suspicion of even a visionary self-interest, even as she was pure in senses more obvious — never once did this holy child, as regarded herself, relax from her belief in the darkness that was travelling to meet her. She might not prefigure the very manner of her death; she saw not in vision, perhaps, the aërial altitude of the fiery scaffold, the spectators without end on every road pouring into Rouen as to a coronation, the surging smoke, the volleying flames, the hostile faces all around, the pitying eye that lurked but here and there until nature and imperishable truth broke loose from artificial restraints; these might not be apparent through the mists of the hurrying future. But the voice that called her to death, *that* she heard for ever.

Great was the throne of France even in those days, and great was he that sate upon it: but well Joanna knew that not the throne, nor he that sate upon it, was for *her;* but, on the contrary, that she was for *them;* not she by them, but they by her, should rise from the dust. Gorgeous were the lilies of France, and for centuries had the privilege to spread their beauty over land and sea, until, in another century, the wrath of God and man combined to wither them; but well Joanna knew, early at Domrémy she had read that bitter truth, that the lilies of France would decorate no garland for *her*. Flower nor bud, bell nor blossom, would ever bloom for *her*.

But stop. What reason is there for taking up this subject of Joanna precisely in the spring of 1847?

Might it not have been left till the spring of 1947? or, perhaps, left till called for? Yes, but it *is* called for; and clamorously. You are aware, reader, that amongst the many original thinkers, whom modern France has produced, one of the reputed leaders is M. Michelet. All these writers are of a revolutionary cast; not in a political sense merely, but in all senses; mad, oftentimes, as March hares; crazy with the laughing-gas of recovered liberty; drunk with the wine-cup of their mighty Revolution, snorting, whinnying, throwing up their heels, like wild horses in the boundless pampas, and running races of defiance with snipes, or with the winds, or with their own shadows, if they can find nothing else to challenge. Some time or other, I, that have leisure to read, may introduce *you*, that have not, to two or three dozen of these writers; of whom I can assure you beforehand that they are often profound, and at intervals are even as impassioned as if they were come of our best English blood, and sometimes (because it is not pleasant that people should be too easy to understand) almost as obscure as if they had been suckled by transcendental German nurses. But now, confining our attention to M. Michelet — who is quite sufficient to lead a man into a gallop, requiring two relays, at least, of fresh readers, — we in England — who know him best by his worst book, the book against Priests, &c., which has been most circulated — know him disadvantageously. That book is a rhapsody of incoherence. M. Michelet was light-headed, I believe, when he wrote it: and it is well that his keepers overtook him in time to intercept a second part. But his *History of France* is quite another thing. A man, in whatsoever craft he sails, cannot stretch away out of sight when he is linked to the windings of the shore by towing ropes of history. Facts, and the consequences of facts, draw the writer back to the falconer's lure from the giddiest heights of speculation. Here, therefore — in his *France* — if not always free from flightiness, if now and then off like a rocket for an airy wheel in the clouds, M. Michelet, with natural politeness, never forgets that he has left a large audience waiting for him on earth, and gazing upwards in anxiety for his return: return, therefore, he does. But History, though clear of certain temptations in one direction, has separate dangers of its own. It is impossible so to write a History of France, or of England — works becoming every hour more indispensable to the inevitably-political man of this day — without perilous openings for assault. If I, for instance, on the part of England, should happen to turn my labors into that channel, and (on the model of Lord Percy going to Chevy Chase) —

——— 'A vow to God should make
My pleasure in the Michelet woods
Three summer days to take,'

— probably from simple delirium, I might hunt M. Michelet into *delirium tremens*. Two strong angels stand by the side of History, whether French History or English, as heraldic supporters: the angel of Research on the left hand, that must read millions of dusty parchments, and of pages blotted with lies; the angel of Meditation on the right hand, that must cleanse these lying records with fire, even as of old the draperies of *asbestos* were cleansed, and must quicken them into regenerated life. Willingly I acknowledge that no man will ever avoid innumerable errors of detail: with so vast a compass of ground to traverse, this is impossible: but such errors (though I have a bushel on hand, at M. Michelet's service) are not the game I chase: it is the bitter and unfair spirit in which M. Michelet writes against England. Even *that*, after all, is but my secondary object: the real one is Joanna, the Pucelle d'Orleans for herself.

I am not going to write the History of *La Pucelle:* to do this, or even circumstantially to report the history of her persecution and bitter death, of her struggle with false witnesses and with ensnaring judges, it would be necessary to have before us *all* the documents, and, therefore, the collection only now forthcoming in Paris. But *my* purpose is narrower. There have been great thinkers, disdaining the careless judgments of contemporaries, who have thrown themselves boldly on the judgment of a far posterity, that should have had time to review, to ponder, to compare. There have been great actors on the stage of tragic humanity that might, with the same depth of confidence, have appealed from the levity of compatriot friends — too heartless for the sublime interest of their story, and too impatient for the labor of sifting its perplexities — to the magnanimity and justice of enemies. To this class belongs the Maid of Arc. The Romans were too faithful to the ideal of grandeur in themselves not to relent, after a generation or two, before the grandeur of Hannibal. Mithridates — a more doubtful person — yet, merely for the magic perseverance of his indomitable malice, won from the same Romans the only real honor that ever he received on earth. And we English have ever shown the same homage to stubborn enmity. To work unflinchingly for the ruin of England ; to say through life, by word and by deed — *Delenda est Anglia Victrix !* that one purpose of malice, faithfully pursued, has quartered some people upon our national funds of homage as by a perpetual annuity. Better than an inheritance of service rendered to England herself, has sometimes proved the most insane hatred to England. Hyder Ali, even his far inferior son Tippoo, and Napoleon, have all benefited by this disposition amongst ourselves to exaggerate the merit of diabolic enmity. Not one of these men was ever capable, in a solitary instance, of praising an enemy — [what do you say to *that*, reader ?] and yet in *their* behalf, we consent to forget, not their crimes only, but (which is worse) their hideous bigotry and anti-magnanimous egotism ; for nationality it was not. Suffrein, and some half dozen of other French nautical heroes, because rightly they did us all the mischief they could, [which was really great] are names justly reverenced in England. On the same principle, La Pucelle d'Orleans, the victorious enemy of England, has been destined to receive her deepest commemoration from the magnanimous justice of Englishmen.

Joanna, as we in England should call her, but, according to her own statement, Jeanne (or, as M. Michelet asserts, Jean[3]) d'Arc, was born at Domrémy, a village on the marshes of Lorraine and Champagne, and dependent upon the town of Vaucouleurs. I have called her a Lorrainer, not simply because the word is prettier, but because Champagne too odiously reminds us English of what are for *us* imaginary wines, which, undoubtedly, *La Pucelle* tasted as rarely as we English; we English, because the Champagne of London is chiefly grown in Devonshire; *La Pucelle*, because the Champagne of Champagne never, by any chance, flowed into the fountain of Domrémy, from which only she drank. M. Michelet will have her to be a *Champenoise*, and for no better reason than that she 'took after her father,' who happened to be a *Champenoise.* I am sure she did *not:* for her father was a filthy old fellow, whom I shall soon teach the judicious reader to hate. But, (says M. Michelet, arguing the case physiologically) 'she had none of the Lorrainian asperity;' no, it seems she had only 'the gentleness of Champagne, its simplicity mingled with sense and acuteness, as you find it in Joinville.' All these things she had; and she was worth a thousand Joinvilles, meaning either the prince so called, or the fine old crusader. But still, though I love Joanna dearly, I cannot shut my eyes entirely to the Lorraine element of 'asperity' in her nature. No; really now, she must have had a shade of *that*, though very slightly developed — a mere soupçon, as French cooks express it in speaking of cayenne pepper, when she caused so many of our English throats to be cut. But could she do less? No; I always say so; but still you never saw a person kill even a trout with a perfectly 'Champagne' face of 'gentleness and simplicity,' though, often, no doubt, with considerable 'acuteness.' All your cooks and butchers wear a *Lorraine* cast of expression.

These disputes, however, turn on refinements too nice. Domrémy stood upon the frontiers; and, like other frontiers, produced a *mixed* race representing the *cis* and the *trans*. A river (it is true) formed the boundary line at this point — the river Meuse; and *that*, in old days, might have divided the populations; but in these days it did not — there were bridges, there were ferries, and weddings crossed from the right bank to the left. Here lay two great roads, not so much for travellers, that were few, as for armies that were too many by half. These two roads, one of which was the great high road between France and Germany, *decussated* at this very point; which is a learned way of saying that they formed a St. Andrew's cross, or letter X. I hope the compositor will choose a good large X, in which case the point of intersection, the *locus* of conflux for these four diverging arms, will finish the reader's geographical education, by showing him to a hair's breadth where it was that Domrémy stood. These roads, so grandly situated, as great trunk arteries between two mighty realms,[4] and haunted for ever by wars or rumors of wars, decussated (for any thing I know to the contrary) absolutely under Joanna's bedroom window; one rolling away to the right, past Monsieur D'Arc's old barn, and the other unaccountably preferring (but there's no disputing about tastes) to sweep round that odious man's odious pigstye to the left.

Things being situated as is here laid down, viz., in respect of the decussation, and in respect of Joanna's bed-room; it follows that, if she had dropped her glove by accident from her chamber window into the very bull's eye of the target, in the centre of X, not one of several great potentates could (though all animated by the sincerest desires for the peace of Europe) have possibly come to any clear understanding on the question of whom the glove was meant for. Whence the candid reader perceives at once the necessity for at least four bloody wars. Falling indeed a little farther, as, for instance, into the pigstye, the glove could not have furnished to the most peppery prince any shadow of excuse for arming: he would not have had a leg to stand upon in taking such a perverse line of conduct. But, if it fell (as by the hypothesis it did) into the one sole point of ground common to four kings, it is clear that, instead of no leg to stand upon, eight separate legs would have had no ground to stand upon unless by treading on each other's toes. The philosopher, therefore, sees clearly the necessity of a war, and regrets that sometimes nations do not wait for grounds of war so solid.

In the circumstances supposed, though the four kings might be unable to see their way clearly without the help of gunpowder to any decision upon Joanna's intention, she — poor thing! — never could mistake her intentions for a moment. All her love was for France; and, therefore, any glove she might drop into the *quadrivium* must be wickedly missent by the post-office, if it found its way to any king but the king of France.

On whatever side of the border chance had thrown Joanna, the same love to France would have been nurtured. For it is a strange fact, noticed by M. Michelet and others, that the Dukes of Bar and Lorraine had for generations pursued the policy of eternal warfare with France on their own account, yet also of eternal amity and league with France in case anybody else presumed to attack her. Let peace settle upon France, and before long you might rely upon seeing the little vixen Lorraine flying at the throat of France. Let France be assailed by a formidable enemy, and instantly you saw a Duke of Lorraine or Bar insisting on having his throat cut in support of France; which favor accordingly was cheerfully granted to them in three great successive battles by the English and by the Turkish sultan, viz., at Crécy, at Nicopolis, and at Agincourt.

This sympathy with France during great eclipses, in those that during ordinary seasons were always teasing her with brawls and guerilla inroads, strengthened the natural piety to France of those that were confessedly the children of her own house. The outposts of France, as one may call the great frontier provinces, were of all localities the most devoted to the Fleurs de Lys. To witness, at any great crisis, the generous devotion to these lilies of the little fiery cousin that in gentler weather was for ever tilting at her breast, could not but fan the zeal of the legitimate daughter: whilst to occupy a post of honor on the frontiers against an old hereditary enemy of France, would naturally have stimulated this zeal by a sentiment of martial pride, had there even been no other stimulant to zeal by a sense of danger always threatening, and of hatred always smouldering. That great four-headed road was a perpetual memento to patriotic ardor. To say, this way lies the road to Paris — and that other way to Aix-la-Chapelle, this to Prague, that to Vienna — nourished the warfare of the heart by daily ministrations of sense. The eye that watched for the gleams of lance or helmet from the hostile frontier, the ear that listened for the groaning of wheels, made the highroad itself, with its relations to centres so remote, into a manual of patriotic enmity.

The situation, therefore, *locally* of Joanna was full of profound suggestions to a heart that listened for the stealthy steps of change and fear that too surely were in motion. But if the place were grand, the times, the burthen of the times, was far more so. The air overhead in its upper chambers were *hurtling* with the obscure sound; was dark with sullen fermenting of storms that had been gathering for a hundred and thirty years. The battle of Agincourt in Joanna's childhood had re-opened the wounds of France. Crécy and Poietiers, those withering overthrows for the chivalry of France, had been tranquillized by more than half a century; but this resurrection of their trumpet wails made the whole series of battles and endless skirmishes take their stations as parts in one drama. The graves that had closed sixty years ago, seemed to fly open in sympathy with a sorrow that echoed their own. The monarchy of France labored in extremity, rocked and reeled like a ship fighting with the darkness of monsoons. The madness of the poor king (Charles VI.) falling in at such a crisis, like the case of women laboring in childbirth during the storming of a city, trebled the awfulness of the time. Even the wild story of the incident which had immediately occasioned the explosion of this madness — the case of a man unknown, gloomy, and perhaps maniacal himself, coming out of a forest at noon-day, laying his hand upon the bridle of the king's horse, checking him for a moment to say, 'Oh, King, thou art betrayed,' and then vanishing no man knew whither, as he had appeared for no man knew what — fell in with the universal prostration of mind that laid France on her knees as before the slow unweaving of some ancient prophetic doom. The famines, the extraordinary diseases, the insurrections of the peasantry up and down Europe, these were chords struck from the same mysterious harp; but these were transitory chords. There had been others of deeper and more sonorous sound. The termination of the Crusades, the destruction of the Templars, the Papal interdicts, the tragedies caused or suffered by the House of Anjou, by the Emperor — these were full of a more permanent significance; but since then the colossal figure of feudalism was seen standing as it were on tiptoe at Crécy for flight from earth: that was a revolution unparalleled; yet *that* was a trifle by comparison with the more fearful revolutions that were mining below the Church. By her own internal schisms, by the abominable spectacle of a double Pope — so that no man, except through political bias, could even guess which was Heaven's vicegerent, and which the creature of hell — she was already rehearsing, as in still earlier forms she had rehearsed, the first rent in her foundations (reserved for the coming century) which no man should ever heal.

These were the loftiest peaks of the cloudland in the skies, that to the scientific gazer first caught the colors of the *new* morning in advance. But the whole vast range alike of sweeping glooms overhead, dwelt upon all meditative minds, even those that could not distinguish the altitudes nor decipher the forms. It was, therefore, not her own age alone, as affected by its immediate calamities, that lay with such weight upon Joanna's mind; but her own age, as one section in a vast mysterious drama, unweaving through a century back, and drawing nearer continually to crisis after crisis. Cataracts and rapids were heard roaring ahead; and signs were seen far back, by help of old men's memories, which answered secretly to signs now coming forward on the eye, even as locks answer to keys. It was not wonderful that in such a haunted solitude, with such a haunted heart, Joanna should see angelic visions, and hear angelic voices. These voices whispered to her the duty imposed upon herself, of delivering France. Five years she listened to these monitory voices with internal struggles. At length she could resist no longer. Doubt gave way; and she left her home in order to present herself at the Dauphin's court.

The education of this poor girl was mean according to the present standard: was ineffably grand, according to a purer philosophic standard: and only not good for our age, because for us it would be unattainable. She read nothing, for she could not read; but she had heard others read parts of the Roman martyrology. She wept in sympathy with the sad *Misereres* of the Romish chanting; she rose to heaven with the glad triumphant *Gloria in Excelcis:* she drew her comfort and her vital strength from the rites of her church. But, next after these spiritual advantages, she owed most to the advantages of her situation. The fountain of Domrémy was on the brink of a boundless forest; and it was haunted to that degree by fairies that the parish priest (*curé*) was obliged to read mass there once a year, in order to keep them in any decent bounds. Fairies are important, even in a statistical view ; certain weeds mark poverty in the soil, fairies mark its solitude. As surely as the wolf retires before cities, does the fairy sequester herself from the haunts of licensed victuallers. A village is too much for her nervous delicacy : at most, she can tolerate a distant view of a hamlet. We may judge, therefore, by the uneasiness and extra trouble which they gave to the parson, in what strength the fairies mustered at Domrémy, and, by a satisfactory consequence, how thinly sown with men and women must have been that region even in its inhabited spots. But the forests of Domrémy — those were the glories of the land : for, in them abode mysterious powers and ancient secrets that towered into tragic strength. 'Abbeys there were, and abbey windows, dim and dimly seen — as Moorish temples of the Hindoos,' that exercised even princely power both in Lorraine and in the German Diets. These had their sweet bells that pierced the forests for many a league at matins or vespers, and each its own dreamy legend. Few enough, and scattered enough, were these abbeys, in no degree to disturb the deep solitude of the region ; many enough to spread a network or awning of Christian sanctity over what else might have seemed a heathen wilderness. This sort of religious talisman being secured, a man the most afraid of ghosts (like myself, suppose, or the reader) becomes armed into courage to wander for days in their sylvan recesses. The mountains of the Vosges on the eastern frontier of France, have never attracted much notice from Europe, except in 1813–14 for a few brief months, when they fell within Napoleon's line of defence against the Allies. But they are interesting for this, amongst other features — that they do not, like some loftier ranges, repel woods: the forests and they are on sociable terms. *Live and let live* is their motto. For this reason, in part, these tracts in Lorraine were a favorite hunting ground with the Carlovingian princes. About six hundred years before Joanna's childhood, Charlemagne was known to have hunted there. That, of itself, was a grand incident in the traditions of a forest or a chase. In these vast forests, also, were to be found (if the race was not extinct) those mysterious fawns that tempted solitary hunters into visionary and perilous pursuits. Here was seen, at intervals, that ancient stag who was already nine hundred years old, at the least, but possibly a hundred or two more, when met by Charlemagne; and the thing was put beyond doubt by the inscription upon his golden collar. I believe Charlemagne knighted the stag; and, if ever he is met again by a king, he ought to be made an earl — or, being upon the marches of France, a marquess. Observe, I don't absolutely vouch for all these things: my own opinion varies. On a fine breezy forenoon I am audaciously sceptical; but as twilight sets in, my credulity becomes equal to anything that could be desired. And I have heard candid sportsmen declare that, outside of these very forests near the Vosges, they laughed loudly at all the dim tales connected with their haunted solitudes; but, on reaching a spot notoriously eighteen miles deep within them, they agreed with Sir Roger de Coverley that a good deal might be said on both sides.

Such traditions, or any others that (like the stag) connect distant generations with each other, are, for that cause, sublime; and the sense of the shadowy, connected with such appearances that reveal themselves or not according to circumstances, leaves a coloring of sanctity over ancient forests, even in those minds that utterly reject the legend as a fact.

But, apart from all distinct stories of that order, in any solitary frontier between two great empires, as here, for instance, or in the desert between Syria and the Euphrates, there is an inevitable tendency, in minds of any deep sensibility, to people the solitudes with phantom images of powers that were of old so vast. Joanna, therefore, in her quiet occupation of a shepherdess, would be led continually to brood over the political condition of her country, by the traditions of the past no less than by the mementoes of the local present.

M. Michelet, indeed, says that La Pucelle was *not* a shepherdess. I beg his pardon: she *was*. What he rests upon, I guess pretty well: it is the evidence of a woman called Haumette, the most confidential friend of Joanna. Now, she is a good witness, and a good girl, and I like her; for she makes a natural and affectionate report of Joanna's ordinary life. But still, however good she may be as a witness, Joanna is better; and she, when speaking to the Dauphin, calls herself in the Latin report *Bergereta*. Even Haumette confesses that Joanna tended sheep in her girlhood. And I believe, that, if Miss Haumette were taking coffee alone with me this very evening (February 12, 1847) — in which there would be no subject for scandal or for maiden blushes, because I am an intense philosopher, and Miss H. would be hard upon four hundred and fifty years old — she would admit the following comment upon her evidence to be right. A Frenchman, about thirty years ago, M. Simond, in his *Travels*, mentioned incidentally the following hideous scene as one steadily observed and watched by himself in France at a period some trifle before the French Revolution: — A peasant was ploughing; and the team that drew his plough was a donkey and a woman. Both were regularly harnessed: both pulled alike. This is bad enough; but the Frenchman adds, that, in distributing his lashes, the peasant was obviously desirous of being impartial: or, if either of the yoke-fellows had a right to complain, certainly it was not the donkey. Now, in any country, where such degradation of females could be tolerated by the state of manners, a woman of delicacy would shrink from acknowledging, either for herself or her friend, that she had ever been addicted to any mode of labor not strictly domestic; because, if once owning herself a prædial servant, she would be sensible that this confession extended by probability in the hearer's thoughts to having incurred indignities of this horrible kind. Haumette clearly thinks it more dignified for Joanna to have been darning the stockings of her horny-hoofed father, Monsieur D'Arc, than keeping sheep, lest she might then be suspected of having ever done something worse. But, luckily, there was no danger of *that:* Joanna never was in service; and my opinion is that her father should have mended his own stockings, since probably he was the party to make the holes in them, as many a better man than D'Arc does;

meaning by *that* not myself, because, though certainly a better man than D'Arc, I protest against doing anything of the kind. If I lived even with Friday in Juan Fernandez, either Friday must do all the darning, or else it must go undone. The better men that I meant were the sailors in the British navy, every man of whom mends his own stockings. Who else is to do it? Do you suppose, reader, that the junior lords of the admiralty are under articles to darn for the navy?

The reason, meantime, for my systematic hatred of D'Arc is this. There was a story current in France before the Revolution, framed to ridicule the pauper aristocracy, who happened to have long pedigrees and short rent rolls, viz., that a head of such a house, dating from the Crusades, was overheard saying to his son, a Chevalier of St. Louis, '*Chevalier, as-tu donné au cochon à manger!*' Now, it is clearly made out by the surviving evidence, that D'Arc would much have preferred continuing to say — '*Ma fille as-tu donné au cochon à manger?*' to saying '*Pucelle d'Orléans, as-tu sauvé les fleurs-de-lys?*' There is an old English copy of verses which argues thus: —

'If the man, that turnips cries,
Cry not when his father dies —
Then 'tis plain the man had rather
Have a turnip than his father.'

I cannot say that the logic of these verses was ever *entirely* to my satisfaction. I do not see my way through it as clearly as could be wished. But I see my way most clearly through D'Arc; and the result is — that he would greatly have preferred not merely a turnip to his father, but the saving a pound or so of bacon to saving the Oriflamme of France.

It is probable (as M. Michelet suggests) that the title of Virgin, or *Pucelle*, had in itself, and apart from the miraculous stories about her, a secret power over the rude soldiery and partisan chiefs of that period; for, in such a person, they saw a representative manifestation of the Virgin Mary, who, in a course of centuries, had grown steadily upon the popular heart.

As to Joanna's supernatural detection of the Dauphin (Charles VII.) amongst three hundred lords and knights, I am surprised at the credulity which could ever lend itself to that theatrical juggle. Who admires more than myself the sublime enthusiasm, the rapturous faith in herself, of this pure creature? But I admire not stage artifices, which not *La Pucelle*, but the Court, must have arranged; nor can surrender myself a dupe to a conjuror's *leger-de-main*, such as may be seen every day for a shilling. Southey's 'Joan of Arc' was published in 1796. Twenty years after, talking with Southey, I was surprised to find him still owning a secret bias in favor of Joan, founded on her detection of the Dauphin. The story, for the benefit of the reader new to the case, was this: — *La Pucelle* was first made known to the Dauphin, and presented to his court, at Chinon: and here came her first trial. She was to find out the royal personage amongst the whole ark of clean and unclean creatures. Failing in this *coup d'essai*, she would not simply disappoint many a beating heart in the glittering crowd that on different motives yearned for her success, but she would ruin herself — and, as the oracle within had told her, would ruin France. Our own sovereign lady Victoria rehearses annually a trial not so severe in degree, but the same in kind. She 'pricks' for sheriffs. Joanna pricked for a king. But observe the difference: our own lady pricks for two men out of three; Joanna for one man out of three hundred. Happy Lady of the islands and the orient! — she *can* go astray in her choice only by one half; to the extent of one half she *must* have the satisfaction of being right. And yet, even with these tight limits to the misery of a boundless discretion, permit me, liege Lady, with all loyalty, to submit — that now and then you prick with your pin the wrong man. But the poor child from Domrémy, shrinking under the gaze of a dazzling court — not because dazzling (for in visions she had seen those that were more so,) but because some of them wore a scoffing smile on their features — how should *she* throw her line into so deep a river to angle for a king, where many a gay creature was sporting that masqueraded as kings in dress? Nay, even more than any true king would have done: for, in Southey's version of the story, the Dauphin says, by way of trying the virgin's magnetic sympathy with royalty,

> ——— 'on the throne,
> I the while mingling with the menial throng,
> Some courtier shall be seated.'

This usurper is even crowned: 'the jewell'd crown shines on a menial's head.' But really, that is '*un peu fort;*' and the mob of spectators might raise a scruple whether our friend the jackdaw upon the throne, and the Dauphin himself, were not grazing the shins of treason. For the Dauphin could not lend more than belonged to him. According to the popular notion, he had no crown for himself, but, at most, a *petit écu*, worth thirty pence ; consequently none to lend, on any pretence whatever, until the consecrated Maid should take him to Rheims. This was the *popular* notion in France. The same notion as to the indispensableness of a coronation prevails widely in England. But, certainly, it was the Dauphin's interest to support the popular notion, as he meant to use the services of Joanna. For, if he were king already, what was it that she could do for him beyond Orleans ? And above all, if he were king without a coronation, and without the oil from the sacred ampulla, what advantage was yet open to him by celerity above his competitor the English boy ? Now was to be a race for a coronation : he that should win *that* race, carried the superstition of France along with him. Trouble us not, lawyer, with your quillets. We are illegal blockheads ; so thoroughly without law, that we don't know even if we have a right to be blockheads ; and our mind is made up — that the first man drawn from the oven of coronation at Rheims, is the man that is baked into a king. All others are counterfeits, made of base Indian meal, damaged by sea-water.

La Pucelle, before she could be allowed to practise as a warrior, was put through her manual and platoon exercise, as a juvenile pupil in divinity, before six eminent men in wigs. According to Southey (v. 393, Book III., in the original edition of his 'Joan of Arc') she 'appall'd the doctors.' It's not easy to do *that :* but they had some reason to feel bothered, as that surgeon would assuredly feel bothered, who upon proceeding to dissect a subject, should find the subject retaliating as a dissector upon himself, especially if

Joanna ever made the speech to them which occupies v. 354–391, B. III. It is a double impossibility; 1st, because a piracy from Tindal's *Christianity as old as the Creation:* now a piracy *à parte post* is common enough; but a piracy *à parte ante*, and by three centuries, would (according to our old English phrase[5]) drive a coach-and-six through any copyright act that man born of woman could frame. 2dly, it is quite contrary to the evidence on Joanna's trial; for Southey's 'Joan' of A. Dom. 1796 (Cottle, Bristol), tells the doctors, amongst other secrets, that she never in her life attended — 1st, Mass; nor 2d, the Sacramental table; nor 3d, Confession. Here's a precious windfall for the doctors; they, by snaky tortuosities, had hoped, through the aid of a corkscrew, (which every D. D. or S. T. P. is said to carry in his pocket,) for the happiness of ultimately extracting from Joanna a few grains of heretical powder or small shot, which might have justified their singeing her a little. And just at such a crisis, expressly to justify their burning her to a cinder, up gallops Joanna with a brigade of guns, unlimbers, and serves them out with heretical grape and deistical round-shot enough to lay a kingdom under interdict Any miracles, to which Joanna might treat the grim D. Ds. after *that*, would go to the wrong side of her little account in the clerical books. Joanna would be created a *Dr.* herself, but not of Divinity. For in the Joanna page of the ledger the entry would be — 'Miss Joanna, in acct. with the Church, *Dr.* by sundry diabolic miracles, she having publicly preached heresy, shown herself a witch, and even tried hard to corrupt the principles of six church pillars.' In the mean time, all this deistical confession of Joanna's, besides being suicidal for the interest of her cause, is opposed to the depositions upon *both* trials. The very best witness called from first to last deposes that Joanna attended these rites of her Church even too often; was taxed with doing so; and, by blushing, owned the charge as a fact, though certainly not as a fault. Joanna was a girl of natural piety, that saw God in forests, and hills, and fountains; but did not the less seek him in chapels and consecrated oratories.

This peasant girl was self-educated through her own natural meditativeness. If the reader turns to that divine passage in *Paradise Regained*, which Milton has put into the mouth of our Saviour when first entering the wilderness, and musing upon the tendency of those great impulses growing within himself —

> 'Oh, what a multitude of thoughts arise!' &c.

he will have some notion of the vast reveries which brooded over the heart of Joanna in early girlhood, when the wings were budding that should carry her from Orleans to Rheims; when the golden chariot was dimly revealing itself that should carry her from the kingdom of *France Delivered* to the eternal kingdom.

It is not requisite, for the honor of Joanna, nor is there, in this place, room to pursue her brief career of *action*. That, though wonderful, forms the earthly part of her story: the intellectual part is, the saintly passion of her imprisonment, trial, and execution. It is unfortunate, therefore, for Southey's 'Joan of Arc,' (which however should always be regarded as a *juvenile* effort,) that, precisely when her real glory begins, the poems ends. But this limitation of the interest grew, no doubt, from the constraint inseparably attached to the law of epic unity. Joanna's history bisects into two opposite hemispheres, and both could not have been presented to the eye in one poem, unless by sacrificing all unity of theme, or else by involving the earlier half, as a narrative episode, in the latter; — this might have been done — it might have been communicated to a fellow-prisoner, or a confessor, by Joanna herself, in the same way that Virgil has contrived to acquaint the reader, through the hero's mouth, with earlier adventures that, if told by the poet speaking in his own person, would have destroyed the unity of his fable. The romantic interest of the early and *irrelate* incidents (last night of Troy, &c.) is thrown as an affluent into the general river of the personal narrative, whilst yet the capital current of the *epos*, as unfolding the origin and *incunabula* of Rome, is not for a moment suffered to be modified by events so subordinate and so obliquely introduced. It is sufficient, as concerns *this* section of Joanna's life to say — that she fulfilled, to the height of her promises, the restoration of the prostrate throne. France had become a province of England; and for the ruin of both, if such a yoke could be maintained. Dreadful pecuniary exhaustion caused the English energy to droop; and that critical opening *La Pucelle* used with a corresponding felicity of audacity and suddenness (that were in themselves portentous) for introducing the wedge of French native resources, for rekindling the national pride, and for planting the Dauphin once more upon his feet. When Joanna appeared, he had been on the point of giving up the struggle with the English, distressed as they were, and of flying to the south of France. She taught him to blush for such abject counsels. She liberated Orleans, that great city, so decisive by its fate for the issue of the war, and then beleaguered by the English with an elaborate application of engineering skill unprecedented in Europe. Entering the city after sunset, on the 29th of April, she sang mass on Sunday, May 8, for the entire disappearance of the besieging force. On the 29th of June, she fought and gained over the English the decisive battle of Patay; on the 9th of July, she took Troyes by a coup-de-main from a mixed garrison of English and Burgundians; on the 15th of that month, she carried the Dauphin into Rheims; on Sunday the 17th, she crowned him; and there she rested from her labor of triumph. What remained was — to suffer.

All this forward movement was her own: excepting one man, the whole council was against her. Her enemies were all that drew power from earth. Her supporters were her own strong enthusiasm, and the headlong contagion by which she carried this sublime frenzy into the hearts of women, of soldiers, and of all who lived by labor. Henceforwards she was thwarted; and the worst error, that she committed, was to lend the sanction of her presence to counsels which she disapproved. But she had accomplished the capital objects which her own visions had dictated. These involved all the rest. Errors were now less important; and doubtless it had now become more difficult for herself to pronounce authentically what *were* errors. The noble girl had achieved, as by a rapture of motion, the capital end of clearing out a free space around her sovereign, giving him the power to move his arms with effect; and, secondly, the inappreciable end of winning for that sovereign what seemed to all France the heavenly ratification of his rights, by crowning him with the ancient solemnities. She had made it impossible for the English now to step before her. They were caught in an irretrievable blunder, owing partly to discord amongst the uncles of Henry VI., partly to a want of funds, but partly to the very impossibility which they believed to press with tenfold force upon any French attempt to forestall theirs. They laughed at such a thought; and whilst they laughed, she *did* it. Henceforth the single redress for the English of this capital oversight, but which never *could* have redressed it effectually, was — to vitiate and taint the coronation of Charles VII. as the work of a witch. That policy, and not malice, (as M. Michelet is so happy to believe,) was the moving principle in the subsequent prosecution of Joanna. Unless they unhinged the force of the first coronation in the popular mind, by associating it with power given from hell, they felt that the sceptre of the invader was broken.

But she, the child that, at nineteen, had wrought wonders so great for France, was she not elated? Did she not lose, as men so often *have* lost, all sobriety of mind when standing upon the pinnacle of success so giddy? Let her enemies declare. During the progress of her movement, and in the centre of ferocious struggles, she had manifested the temper of her feelings by the pity which she had every where expressed for the suffering enemy. She forwarded to the English leaders a touching invitation to unite with the French, as brothers, in a common crusade against infidels, thus opening the road for a soldierly retreat. She interposed to protect the captive or the wounded — she mourned over the excesses of her countrymen — she threw herself off her horse to kneel by the dying English soldier, and to comfort him with such ministrations, physical or spiritual, as his situation allowed. 'Nolebat,' says the evidence, 'uti ense suo, aut quemquam interficere.' She sheltered the English, that invoked her aid, in her own quarters. She wept as she beheld, stretched on the field of battle, so many brave enemies that had died without confession. And, as regarded herself, her elation expressed itself thus: — on the day when she had finished her work, she wept; for she knew that, when her task was done, her end must be approaching. Her aspirations pointed only to a place, which seemed to her more than usually full of natural piety, as one in which it would give her pleasure to die. And she uttered, between smiles and tears, as a wish that inexpressibly fascinated her heart, and yet was half fantastic, a broken prayer that God would return her to the solitudes from which he had drawn her, and suffer her to become a shepherdess once more. It was a natural prayer, because nature has laid a necessity upon every human heart to seek for rest, and to shrink from torment. Yet, again, it was a half-fantastic prayer, because, from childhood upwards, visions that she had no power to mistrust, and the voices which sounded in her ear for ever, had long since persuaded her mind, that for *her* no such prayer could be granted. Too well she felt that her mission must be worked out to the end, and that the end was now at hand. All went wrong from this time. She herself had created the *funds* out of which the French restoration should grow; but she was not suffered to witness their development, or their prosperous application. More than one military plan was entered upon which she did not approve. But she still continued to expose her person as before. Severe wounds had not taught her caution. And at length, in a sortie from Compeigne, whether through treacherous collusion on the part of her own friends is doubtful to this day, she was made prisoner by the Burgundians, and finally surrendered to the English.

Now came her trial. This trial, moving of course under English influence, was conducted in chief by the Bishop of Beauvais. He was a Frenchman, sold to English interests, and hoping, by favor of the English leaders, to reach the highest preferment. *Bishop that art*, *Archbishop that shalt be*, *Cardinal that mayest be*, were the words that sounded continually in his ear; and doubtless, a whisper of visions still higher, of a triple crown, and feet upon the necks of kings, sometimes stole into his heart. M. Michelet is anxious to keep us in mind that this Bishop was but an agent of the English. True. But it does not better the case for his countryman; that, being an accomplice in the crime, making himself the leader in the persecution against the helpless girl, he was willing to be all this in the spirit, and with the conscious vileness of a catspaw. Never from the foundations of the earth was there such a trial as this, if it were laid open in all its beauty of defence, and all its hellishness of attack. Oh, child of

France! shepherdess, peasant girl! trodden under foot by all around thee, how I honor thy flashing intellect, quick as God's lightning, and true as that lightning to its mark, that ran before France and laggard Europe by many a century, confounding the malice of the ensnarer, and making dumb the oracles of falsehood! Is it not scandalous, is it not humiliating to civilization, that, even at this day, France exhibits the horrid spectacle of judges examining the prisoner against himself; seducing him, by fraud, into treacherous conclusions against his own head; using the terrors of their power for extorting confessions from the frailty of hope; nay, (which is worse,) using the blandishments of condescension and snaky kindness for thawing into compliances of gratitude those whom they had failed to freeze into terror? Wicked judges! Barbarian jurisprudence! that, sitting in your own conceit on the summits of social wisdom, have yet failed to learn the first principles of criminal justice; sit ye humbly and with docility at the feet of this girl from Domrémy, that tore your webs of cruelty into shreds and dust. 'Would you examine me as a witness against myself?' was the question by which many times she defied their arts. Continually she showed that their interrogations were irrelevant to any business before the court, or that entered into the ridiculous charges against her. General questions were proposed to her on points of casuistical divinity; two-edged questions which not one of themselves could have answered without, on the one side, landing himself in heresy, (as then interpreted,) or, on the other, in some presumptuous expression of self-esteem. Next came a wretched Dominican that pressed her with an objection, which, if applied to the Bible, would tax every one of its miracles with unsoundness. The monk had the excuse of never having read the Bible. M. Michelet has no such excuse; and it makes one blush for him, as a philosopher, to find him describing such an argument as 'weighty,' whereas it is but a varied expression of rude Mahometan metaphysics. Her answer to this, if there were room to place the whole in a clear light, was as shattering as it was rapid. Another thought to entrap her by asking what language the angelic visitors of her solitude had talked; as though heavenly counsels could want polyglott interpreters for every word, or that God needed language at all in whispering thoughts to a human heart. Then came a worse devil, who asked her whether the archangel Michael had appeared naked. Not comprehending the vile insinuation, Joanna, whose poverty suggested to her simplicity that it might be the *costliness* or suitable robes which caused the demur, asked them if they fancied God, who clothed the flowers of the valleys, unable to find raiment for his servants. The answer of Joanna moves a smile of tenderness, but the disappointment of her judges makes one laugh horribly. Others succeeded by troops, who upbraided her with leaving her father; as if that greater Father, whom she believed herself to have been serving, did not retain the power of dispensing with his own rules, or had not said, that, for a less cause than martyrdom, man and woman should leave both father and mother.

On Easter Sunday, when the trial had been long proceeding, the poor girl fell so ill as to cause a belief that she had been poisoned. It was not poison. Nobody had any interest in hastening a death so certain. M. Michelet, whose sympathies with all feelings are so quick that one would gladly see them always as justly directed, reads the case most truly. Joanna had a two-fold malady. She was visited by a paroxysm of the complaint called *home-sickness;* the cruel nature of her imprisonment, and its length, could not but point her solitary thoughts, in darkness, and in chains, (for chained she was,) to Domrémy. And the season, which was the most heavenly period of the spring, added stings to this yearning. That was one of her maladies — *nostalgia*, as medicine calls it; the other was weariness and exhaustion from daily combats with malice. She saw that everybody hated her, and thirsted for her blood; nay, many kind-hearted creatures that would have pitied her profoundly as regarded all political charges, had their natural feelings warped by the belief that she had dealings with fiendish powers. She knew she was to die; that was *not* the misery; the misery was that this consummation could not be reached without so much intermediate strife, as if she were contending for some chance (where chance was none) of happiness, or were dreaming for a moment of escaping the inevitable. Why, then, *did* she contend? Knowing that she would reap nothing from answering her persecutors, why did she not retire by silence from the superfluous contest? It was because her quick and eager loyalty to truth would not suffer her to see it darkened by frauds, which *she* could expose, but others, even of candid listeners, perhaps, could not; it was through that imperishable grandeur of soul, which taught her to submit meekly and without a struggle to her punishment, but taught her *not* to submit — no, not for a moment — to calumny as to facts, or to misconstruction as to motives. Besides, there were secretaries all around the court taking down her words. That was meant for no good to *her*. But the end does not always correspond to the meaning. And Joanna might say to herself — these words that will be used against me to-morrow and the next day, perhaps in some nobler generation may rise again for my justification. Yes, Joanna, they *are* rising even now in Paris, and for more than justification.

Woman, sister — there are some things which you do not execute as well as your brother, man; no, nor ever will. Pardon me if I doubt whether you will ever produce a great poet from your choirs, or a Mozart, or a Phidias, or a Michael Angelo, or a great philosopher, or a great scholar. By which last is meant — not one who depends simply on an infinite memory, but also on an infinite and electrical power of combination; bringing together from the four winds, like the angel of the resurrection, what else were dust from dead men's bones, into the unity of breathing life. If you *can* create yourselves into any of these great creators, why have you not? Do not ask me to say otherwise; because if you do, you will lead me into temptation. For I swore early in life never to utter a falsehood, and, above all, a sycophantic falsehood; and, in the false homage of the modern press towards women, there is horrible sycophancy. It is as hollow, most of it, and it is as fleeting, as is the love that lurks in *uxoriousness*. Yet, if a woman asks me to tell a falsehood, I have long made up my mind — that on moral considerations

I *will* and *ought* to do so, whether it be for any purpose of glory to *her*, or of screening her foibles (for she *does* commit a few), or of humbly, as a vassal, paying a peppercorn rent to her august privilege of caprice. Barring these cases, I must adhere to my resolution of telling no fibs. And I repeat, therefore, but not to be rude, I repeat in Latin —

> Excudent alii meliùs spirantia signa,
> Credo equidem vivos ducent de marmore vultus :
> Altius ascendent : at tu caput, Eva, memento
> Sandalo ut infringas referenti oracula tanta.[6]

Yet, sister woman — though I cannot consent to find a Mozart or a Michael Angelo in your sex, until that day when you claim my promise as to falsehood — cheerfully, and with the love that burns in depths of admiration, I acknowledge that you can do one thing as well as the best of us men — a greater thing than even Mozart is known to have done, or Michael Angelo — you can die grandly, and as goddesses would die were goddesses mortal. If any distant world (which *may* be the case) are so far ahead of us Tellurians in optical resources as to see distinctly through their telescopes all that we do on earth, what is the grandest sight to which we ever treat them ? St. Peter's at Rome, do you fancy, on Easter Sunday, or Luxor, or perhaps the Himalayas ? Pooh ! pooh ! my friend : suggest something better ; these are baubles to *them ;* they see in other worlds, in their own, far better toys of the same kind. These, take my word for it, are nothing. Do you give it up ? The finest thing, then, we have to show them is a scaffold on the morning of execution. I assure you there is a strong muster in those fair telescopic worlds, on any such morning, of those who happen to find themselves occupying the right hemisphere for a peep at *us*. Telescopes look up in the market on that morning, and bear a monstrous premium; for they cheat, probably, in those scientific worlds as well as we do. How, then, if it be announced in some such telescopic world by those who make a livelihood of catching glimpses at our newspapers, whose language they have long since deciphered, that the poor victim in the morning's sacrifice is a woman? How, if it be published on that distant world that the sufferer wears upon her head, in the eyes of many, the garlands of martyrdom? How, if it should be some Marie Antoinette, the widowed queen, coming forward on the scaffold, and presenting to the morning air her head, turned gray prematurely by sorrow, daughter of Cæsars kneeling down humbly to kiss the guillotine, as one that worships death? How, if it were the 'martyred wife of Roland,' uttering impassioned truth — truth odious to the rulers of her country — with her expiring breath? How, if it were the noble Charlotte Corday, that in the bloom of youth, that with the loveliest of persons, that with homage waiting upon her smiles wherever she turned her face to scatter them — homage that followed those smiles as surely as the carols of birds, after showers in spring, follow the re-appearing sun and the racing of sunbeams over the hills — yet thought all these things cheaper than the dust upon her sandals in comparison of deliverance from hell for her dear suffering France? Ah! these were spectacles indeed for those sympathizing people in distant worlds; and some, perhaps, would suffer a sort of martyrdom themselves, because they could not testify their wrath, could not bear witness to the strength of love, and to the fury of hatred, that burned within them at such scenes; could not gather into golden urns some of that glorious dust which rested in the catacombs of earth.

On the Wednesday after Trinity Sunday in **1431**, being then about nineteen years of age, the Maid of Arc underwent her martyrdom. She was conducted before mid-day, guarded by eight hundred spearmen, to a platform of prodigious height, constructed of wooden billets supported by occasional walls of lath and plaster, and traversed by hollow spaces in every direction for the creation of air-currents. The pile 'struck terror,' says M. Michelet, 'by its height;' and, as usual, the English purpose in this is viewed as one of pure malignity. But there are two ways of explaining all that. It is probable that the purpose was merciful. On the circumstances of the execution I shall not linger. Yet, to mark the almost fatal felicity of M. Michelet in finding out whatever may injure the English name, at a moment when every reader will be interested in Joanna's personal appearance, it is really edifying to notice the ingenuity by which he draws into light from a dark corner a very unjust account of it, and neglects, though lying upon the high road, a very pleasing one. Both are from English pens. Grafton, a chronicler but little read, being a stiff-necked John Bull, thought fit to say, that no wonder Joanna should be a virgin, since her 'foule face' was a satisfactory solution of that particular merit. Holinshead, on the other hand, a chronicler somewhat later, every way more important, and universally read, has given a very pleasing testimony to the interesting character of Joanna's person and engaging manners. Neither of these men lived till the following century, so that personally this evidence is none at all. Grafton sullenly and carelessly believed as he wished to believe; Holinshead took pains to inquire, and reports undoubtedly the general impression of France. But I cite the case as illustrating M. Michelet's candor.[7]

The circumstantial incidents of the execution, unless with more space than I can now command, I should be unwilling to relate. I should fear to injure, by imperfect report, a martyrdom which to myself appears so unspeakably grand. Yet for a purpose pointing, not at Joanna but at M. Michelet, — viz., to convince him that an Englishman is capable of thinking more highly of *La Pucelle* than even her admiring countryman, I shall, in parting, allude to one or two traits in Joanna's demeanor on the scaffold, and to one or two in that of the bystanders, which authorize me in questioning an opinion of his upon this martyr's firmness. The reader ought to be reminded that Joanna d'Arc was subjected to an unusually unfair trial of opinion. Any of the elder Christian martyrs had not much to fear of *personal* rancor. The martyr was chiefly regarded as the enemy of Cæsar; at times, also, where any knowledge of the Christian faith and morals existed, with the enmity that arises spontaneously in the worldly against the spiritual. But the martyr, though disloyal, was not supposed to be, therefore, anti-national; and still less was *individually* hateful. What was hated (if anything) belonged to his class, not to himself separately. Now Joanna, if hated at all, was hated personally, and in Rouen on national grounds. Hence there would be a certainty of calumny arising against *her*, such as would not affect martyrs in general. That being the case, it would follow of necessity that some people would impute to her a willingness to recant. No innocence could escape *that*. Now, had she really testified this willingness on the scaffold, it would have argued nothing at all but the weakness of a genial nature shrinking from the instant approach of torment. And those will often pity that weakness most, who, in their own persons, would yield to it least. Meantime, there never was a calumny uttered that drew less support from the recorded circumstances. It rests upon no *positive* testimony, and it has a weight of contradicting testimony to stem. And yet, strange to say, M. Michelet, who at times seems to admire the Maid of Arc as much as I do, is the one sole writer amongst her *friends* who lends some countenance to this odious slander. His words are, that, if she did not utter this word *recant* with her lips, she uttered it in her heart. 'Whether she *said* the word is uncertain: but I affirm that she *thought* it.'

Now, I affirm that she did not; not in any sense of the word '*thought*' applicable to the case. Here is France calumniating *La Pucelle:* here is England defending her. M. Michelet can only mean, that, on *à priori* principles, every woman must be presumed liable to such a weakness; that Joanna was a woman; *ergo*, that she was liable to such a weakness. That is, he only supposes her to have uttered the word by an argument which presumes it impossible for anybody to have done otherwise. I, on the contrary, throw the *onus* of the argument not on presumable tendencies of nature, but on the known facts of that morning's execution, as recorded by multitudes. What else, I demand, than mere weight of metal, absolute nobility of deportment, broke the vast line of battle then arrayed against her? What else but her meek, saintly demeanor, won from the enemies, that till now had believed her a witch, tears of rapturous admiration? 'Ten thousand men,' says M. Michelet himself, 'ten thousand men wept;' and of these ten thousand the majority were political enemies knitted together by cords of superstition. What else was it but her constancy, united with her angelic gentleness, that drove the fanatic English soldier — who had sworn to throw a faggot on her scaffold, as *his* tribute of abhorrence, that *did* so, that fulfilled his vow — suddenly to turn away a penitent for life, saying everywhere that he had seen a dove rising upon wings to heaven from the ashes where she had stood? What else drove the executioner to kneel at every shrine for pardon to *his* share in the tragedy? And, if all this were insufficient, then I cite the closing act of her life as valid on her behalf, were all other testimonies against her. The executioner had been directed to apply his torch from below. He did so. The fiery smoke rose upwards in billowing volumes. A Dominican monk was then standing almost at her side. Wrapt up in his sublime office, he saw not the danger, but still persisted in his prayers. Even then, when the last enemy was racing up the fiery stairs to seize her, even at that moment did this noblest of girls think only for *him*, the one friend that would not forsake her, and not for herself; bidding him with her last breath to care for his own preservation, but to leave *her* to God. That girl, whose latest breath ascended in this sublime expression of self-oblivion, did not utter the word *recant* either with her lips or in her heart. No; she did not, though one should rise from the dead to swear it.

* * * * * * * *

Bishop of Beauvais! thy victim died in fire upon a scaffold — thou upon a down bed. But for the departing minutes of life, both are oftentimes alike. At the farewell crisis, when the gates of death are opening, and flesh is resting from its struggles, oftentimes the tortured and the torturer have the same truce from carnal torment; both sink together into sleep; together both, sometimes, kindle into dreams. When the mortal mists were gathering fast upon you two, Bishop and Shepherd girl — when the pavilions of life were closing up their shadowy curtains about you — let us try, through the gigantic glooms, to decipher the flying features of your separate visions.

The shepherd girl that had delivered France — she, from her dungeon, she, from her baiting at the stake, she, from her duel with fire, as she entered her last dream — saw Domrémy, saw the fountain of Domrémy, saw the pomp of forests in which her childhood had wandered. That Easter festival, which man had denied to her languishing heart — that resurrection of spring-time, which the darkness of dungeons had intercepted from *her*, hungering after the glorious liberty of forests — were by God given back into her hands, as jewels that had been stolen from her by robbers. With those, perhaps, (for the minutes of dreams can stretch into ages,) was given back to her by God the bliss of childhood. By special privilege, for *her* might be created, in this farewell dream, a second childhood, innocent as the first; but not, like *that*, sad with the gloom of a fearful mission in the rear. This mission had now been fulfilled. The storm was weathered, the skirts even of that mighty storm were drawing off. The blood, that she was to reckon for, had been exacted; the tears, that she was to shed in secret, had been paid to the last. The hatred to herself in all eyes had been faced steadily, had been suffered, had been survived. And in her last fight upon the scaffold she had triumphed gloriously; victoriously she had tasted the stings of death. For all, except this comfort from her farewell dream, she had died — died, amidst the tears of ten thousand enemies — died, amidst the drums and trumpets of armies — died, amidst peals redoubling upon peals, volleys upon volleys, from the saluting clarions of martyrs.

Bishop of Beauvais! because the guilt-burthened man is in dreams haunted and waylaid by the most frightful of his crimes, and because upon that fluctuating mirror — rising (like the mocking mirrors of *mirage* in Arabian deserts) from the fens of death — most of all are reflected the sweet countenances which the man has laid in ruins; therefore I know, Bishop, that you also, entering your final dream, saw Domrémy. That fountain, of which the witnesses spoke so much, showed itself to your eyes in pure morning dews; but neither dews, nor the holy dawn, could cleanse away the bright spots of innocent blood upon its surface. By the fountain, Bishop, you saw a woman seated, that hid her face. But as *you* draw near, the woman raises her wasted features. Would Domrémy know them again for the features of her child? Ah, but *you* know them, Bishop, well! Oh, mercy! what a groan was *that* which the servants, waiting outside the Bishop's dream at his bedside, heard from his laboring heart, as at this moment he turned away from the fountain and the woman, seeking rest in the forests afar off. Yet not *so* to escape the woman, whom once again he must behold before he dies. In the forests to which he prays for pity, will he find a respite? What a tumult, what a gathering of feet is there! In glades, where only wild deer should run, armies and nations are assembling; towering in the fluctuating crowd are phantoms that belong to departed hours. There is the great English Prince, Regent of France. There is my Lord of Winchester, the princely Cardinal, that died and made no sign. There is the Bishop of Beauvais, clinging to the shelter of thickets. What building is that which hands so rapid are raising? Is it a martyr's scaffold? Will they burn the child of Domrémy a second time? No: it is a tribunal that rises to the clouds; and two nations stand around it, waiting for a trial. Shall my Lord of Beauvais sit again upon the judgment-seat, and again number the hours for the innocent? Ah! no: he is the prisoner at the bar. Already all is waiting; the mighty audience is gathered, the Court is hurrying to their seats, the witnesses are arrayed, the trumpets are sounding, the judge is going to take his place. Oh! but this is sudden. My lord, have you no counsel? 'Counsel I have none: in heaven above, or on earth beneath, counsellor there is none now that would take a brief from *me*: all are silent.' Is it, indeed, come to this? Alas! the time is short, the tumult is wondrous, the crowd stretches away into infinity, but yet I will search in it for somebody to take your brief: I know of somebody that will be your counsel. Who is this that cometh from Domrémy? Who is she that cometh in bloody coronation robes from Rheims? Who is she that cometh with blackened flesh from walking the furnaces of Rouen? This is she, the shepherd girl, counsellor that had none for herself, whom I choose, Bishop, for yours. She it is, I engage, that shall take my lord's brief. She it is, Bishop, that would plead for you: yes, Bishop, SHE — when heaven and earth are silent.

NOTES.

NOTE 1. Page 79.

Arc: — Modern France, that should know a great deal better than myself, insists that the name is not d'Arc, *i. e.* of Arc, but *Darc.* Now it happens sometimes, that if a person, whose position guarantees his access to the best information, will content himself with gloomy dogmatism, striking the table with his fist, and saying in a terrific voice — 'It *is* so; and there's an end of it,' — one bows deferentially, and submits. But if, unhappily for himself, won by this docility, he relents too amiably into reasons and arguments, probably one raises an insurrection against him that may never be crushed; for in the fields of logic one can skirmish, perhaps, as well as he. Had he confined himself to dogmatism; he would have entrenched his position in darkness, and have hidden his own vulnerable points. But coming down to base reasons, he lets in light, and one sees where to plant the blows. Now, the worshipful reason of modern France for disturbing the old received spelling, is — that Jean Hordal, a descendant of *La Pucelle's* brother, spelled the name *Darc,* in 1612. But what of that? Beside the chances that M. Hordal might be a gigantic blockhead, it is notorious that what small matter of spelling Providence had thought fit to disburse amongst man in the seventeenth century, was all monopolized by printers: in France, much more so.

NOTE 2. Page 80.

Those that share thy blood: — a collateral relative of Joanna's was subsequently ennobled by the title of *du Lys.*

NOTE 3. Page 85.

'*Jean.*'—M. Michelet asserts that there was a mystical meaning at that æra in calling a child *Jean;* it implied a secret commendation of a child, if not a dedication, to St. John the Evangelist, the beloved disciple, the apostle of love and mysterious visions. But, really, as the name was so exceedingly common, few people will detect a mystery in calling a *boy* by the name of Jack, though it *does* seem mysterious to call a girl Jack. It may be less so in France, where a beautiful practice has always prevailed of giving to a boy his mother's name — preceded and strengthened by a male name, as *Charles Anne, Victor Victoire.* In cases where a mother's memory has been unusually dear to a son, this vocal memento of her, locked into the circle of his own name, gives to it the tenderness of a testamentary relique, or a funeral ring. I presume, therefore, that *La Pucelle* must have borne the baptismal names of Jeanne Jean; the latter with no reference to so sublime a person as St. John, but simply to some relative.

NOTE 4. Page 87.

And reminding one of that inscription, so justly admired by Paul Richter, which a Russian Czarina placed on a guide-post near Moscow — *This is the road that leads to Constantinople.*

NOTE 5. Page 101.

Yes, old — very old phrase: not as ignoramuses fancy, a phrase recently minted by a Repealer in Ireland.

NOTE 6. Page 112.

Our sisters are always rather uneasy when we say anything of them in Latin or Greek. It is like giving sealed orders to a sea captain, which he is not to open for his life till he comes into a certain latitude, which latitude, perhaps, he never *will* come into, and thus may miss the secret till he is going to the bottom. Generally I acknowledge that it is not polite before our female friends to cite a single word of Latin without instantly translating it. But in this particular case, where I am only iterating a disagreeable truth, they will please to recollect that the politeness lies in *not* translating. However, if they insist absolutely on knowing this very night, before going to bed, what it is that those ill-looking lines contain, I refer them to Dryden's Virgil, somewhere in the 6th Book of the Æneid, except as to the closing line and a half, which contain a private suggestion of my own to discontented nymphs, anxious to see the equilibrium of advantages re-established between the two sexes.

NOTE 7. Page 115.

Amongst the many ebullitions of M. Michelet's fury against us poor English, are four which will be likely to amuse the reader; and they are the more conspicuous in collision with the justice which he sometimes does us, and the very indignant admiration which, under some aspects, he grants to us.

1. Our English literature he admires with some gnashing of teeth. He pronounces it 'fine and sombre,' but, I lament to add, 'sceptical, Judaic, Satanic — in a word, Anti-Christian.' That Lord Byron should figure as a member of this diabolical corporation, will not surprise men. It *will* surprise them to hear that Milton is one of its Satanic leaders. Many are the generous and eloquent Frenchmen, beside Chateaubriand, who have, in the course of the last thirty years, nobly suspended their own burning nationality, in order to render a more rapturous homage at the feet of Milton; and some of them have raised Milton almost to a level with angelic natures. Not one of them has thought of looking for him *below* the earth. As to Shakspeare, M. Michelet detects in him a most extraordinary mare's nest. It is this: he does 'not recollect to have seen the name of God' in any part of his works. On reading such words, it is natural to rub one's eyes, and suspect that all one has ever seen in this world may have been a pure ocular delusion. In particular, I begin myself to suspect that the word '*la gloire*' never occurs in any Parisian journal. 'The great

English nation,' says M. Michelet, 'has one immense profound vice,' to wit, 'pride.' Why, really, that may be true; but we have a neighbor not absolutely clear of an 'immense profound vice,' as like ours in color and shape as cherry to cherry. In short, M. Michelet thinks us, by fits and starts, admirable, only that we are detestable; and he would adore some of our authors, were it not that so intensely he could have wished to kick them.

2. M. Michelet thinks to lodge an arrow in our sides by a very odd remark upon Thomas à Kempis: which is, that a man of any conceivable European blood — a Finlander, suppose, or a Zantiote — might have written Tom; only not an Englishman. Whether an Englishman could have forged Tom, must remain a matter of doubt, unless the thing had been tried long ago. That problem was intercepted for ever by Tom's perverseness in choosing to manufacture himself. Yet, since nobody is better aware than M. Michelet, that this very point of Kempis *having* manufactured Kempis is furiously and hopelessly litigated, three or four nations claiming to have forged his work for him, the shocking old doubt will raise its snaky head once more — whether this forger, who rests in so much darkness, might not, after all, be of English blood. Tom, it may be feared, is known to modern English literature chiefly by an irreverent mention of his name in a line of Peter Pindar's (Dr. Wolcot) fifty years back, where he is described as

'Kempis Tom,
Who clearly shows the way to Kingdom Come.'

Few in these days can have read him, unless in the Methodist version of John Wesley. Amongst those few, however, happens to be myself; which arose from the accident of having, when a boy of eleven, received a copy of the *De Imitatione Christi*, as a bequest from a relation, who died very young; from which cause, and from the external prettiness of the book, being a Glasgow reprint, by the celebrated Foulis, and gaily bound, I was induced to look into it; and finally read it many times over, partly out of some sympathy which, even in those days, I had with its simplicity and devotional fervor ; but much more from the savage delight I found in laughing at Tom's Latinity. *That*, I freely grant to M. Michelet, is inimitable ; else, as regards substance, it strikes me that I could forge a better *De Imitatione* myself. But there is no knowing till one tries. Yet, after all, it is not certain whether the original *was* Latin. But, however *that* may have been, if it is possible that M. Michelet * can be accurate in saying that there are no less than *sixty* French versions (not editions, observe, but separate versions) existing of the *De Imitatione*, how prodigious must have been the adaptation of the book to the religious heart of the fifteenth century ! Excepting the Bible, but excepting *that* only in Protestant lands, no book known to man has had the same distinction. It is the most marvellous bibliographical fact on record.

3. Our English girls, it seems, are as faulty in one way as we English males in another. None of us lads could have written the *Opera Omnia* of Mr. à Kempis ; neither could any of our lasses have assumed male attire like *La Pucelle*. But why? Because, says Michelet, English girls and German think so much of an indecorum. Well, that is a good fault, generally speaking. But M. Michelet ought to have remembered a fact in the martyrologies which justifies both parties,—

* 'If M. Michelet can be accurate.' However, on consideration, this statement does not depend on Michelet. The bibliographer, Barbier, has absolutely *specified* sixty in a separate dissertation, *soixante traductions*, amongst those even that have not escaped the search. The Italian translations are said to be thirty. As to mere *editions*, not counting the early MSS. for half a century before printing was introduced, those in Latin amount to two thousand, and those in French to one thousand. Meantime, it is very clear to me that this astonishing popularity, so entirely unparalleled in literature, could not have existed except in Roman Catholic times, nor subsequently have lingered in any Protestant land. It was the denial of Scripture fountains to thirsty lands which made this slender rill of Scripture truth so passionately welcome.

the French heroine for doing, and the general choir of English girls for *not* doing. A female saint, specially renowned in France, had, for a reason as weighty as Joanna's, viz., expressly to shield her modesty amongst men, wore a male military harness. That reason and that example authorized *La Pucelle;* but our English girls, as a body, have seldom any such reason, and certainly no such saintly example, to plead. This excuses *them.* Yet, still, if it is indispensable to the national character that our young women should now and then trespass over the frontier of decorum, it then becomes a patriotic duty in me to assure M. Michelet that we have such ardent females amongst us, and in a long series — some detected in naval hospitals, when too sick to remember their disguise; some on fields of battle; multitudes never detected at all; some only suspected; and others discharged without noise by war offices and other absurd people. In our navy, both royal and commercial, and generally from deep remembrances of slighted love, women have sometimes served in disguise for many years, taking contentedly their daily allowance of burgoo, biscuit, or cannon balls — anything, in short, digestible or indigestible, that it might please Providence to send. One thing, at least, is to their credit: never any of these poor masks, with their deep silent remembrances, have been detected through murmuring, or what is nautically understood by 'skulking.' So, for once, M. Michelet has an *erratum* to enter upon the fly-leaf of his book in presentation copies.

4. But the last of these ebullitions is the most lively. We English, at Orleans, and after Orleans, (which is not quite so extraordinary, if all were told,) fled before the Maid of Arc. Yes, says M. Michelet, you *did:* deny it, if you can. Deny it, my dear? I don't mean to deny it. Running away, in many cases, is a thing so excellent, that no philosopher would, at times, condescend to adopt any other step. All of us nations in Europe, without one exception, have shown our philosophy in that way at times. Even people, '*qui ne se rendent pas,*' have deigned both to run and to shout, '*Sauve qui peut!*' at odd times of sunset; though, for my part, I have no pleasure in recalling unpleasant remembrances to brave men; and yet,

really, being so philosophic, they ought *not* to be unpleasant. But the amusing feature in M. Michelet's reproach, is the way in which he *improves* and varies against us the charge of running, as if he were singing a catch. Listen to him. They '*showed their backs,*' did these English. (Hip, hip, hurrah! three times three!) '*Behind good walls, they let themselves be taken.*' (Hip, hip! nine times nine!) They '*ran as fast as their legs could carry them.*' (Hurrah! twenty-seven times twenty-seven!) They '*ran before a girl;*' they did. (Hurrah! eighty-one times eighty-one!) This reminds one of criminal indictments on the old model in English courts, where (for fear the prisoner should escape) the crown lawyer varied the charge perhaps through forty counts. The law laid its guns so as to rake the accused at every possible angle. Whilst the indictment was reading, he seemed a monster of crime in his own eyes; and yet, after all, the poor fellow had but committed one offence, and not always *that*. N. B. — Not having the French original at hand, I make my quotations from a friend's copy of Mr. Walter Kelly's translation, which seems to me faithful, spirited, and idiomatically English — liable, in fact, only to the single reproach of occasional provincialisms.

THE ENGLISH MAIL-COACH;

OR,

THE GLORY OF MOTION.

SOME twenty or more years before I matriculated at Oxford, Mr. Palmer, M. P. for Bath, had accomplished two things, very hard to do on our little planet, the Earth, however cheap they may happen to be held by the eccentric people in comets: he had invented mail-coaches, and he had married the daughter[1] of a duke. He was, therefore, just twice as great a man as Galileo, who certainly invented (or *discovered*) the satellites of Jupiter, those very next things extant to mail-coaches in the two capital points of speed and keeping time, but who did *not* marry the daughter of a duke.

These mail-coaches, as organized by Mr. Palmer, are entitled to a circumstantial notice from myself—having had so large a share in developing the anarchies of my subsequent dreams, an agency which they accomplished, first, through velocity, at that time unprecedented; they first revealed the glory of motion: suggesting, at the same time, an under-sense, not unpleasurable, of possible though indefinite danger; secondly, through grand effects for the eye between lamp-light and the darkness upon solitary roads; thirdly, through animal beauty and power so often displayed in the class of horses selected for this mail service; fourthly, through the conscious presence of a central intellect, that, in the midst of vast distances,[2] of storms, of darkness, of night, overruled all obstacles into one steady coöperation in a national result. To my own feeling, this post-office service recalled some mighty orchestra, where a thousand instruments, all disregarding each other, and so far in danger of discord, yet all obedient as slaves to the supreme *baton* of some great leader, terminate in a perfection of harmony like that of heart, veins, and arteries, in a healthy animal organization. But, finally, that particular element in this whole combination which most impressed myself, and through which it is that to this hour Mr. Palmer's mail-coach system tyrannizes by terror and terrific beauty over my dreams, lay in the awful political mission which at that time it fulfilled. The mail-coaches it was that distributed over the face of the land, like the opening of apocalyptic vials, the heart-shaking news of Trafalgar, of Salamanca, of Vittoria, of Waterloo. These were the harvests that, in the grandeur of their reaping, redeemed the tears and blood in which they had been sown. Neither was the meanest peasant so much below the grandeur and the sorrow of the times as to confound these battles, which were gradually moulding the destinies of Christendom, with the vulgar conflicts of ordinary warfare, which are oftentimes but gladiatorial trials of national prowess. The victories of England in this stupendous contest rose of themselves as natural *Te Deums* to heaven; and it was felt by the thoughtful that such victories, at such a crisis of general prostration, were not more beneficial to ourselves than finally to France, and to the nations of western and central Europe, through whose pusillanimity it was that the French domination had prospered.

The mail-coach, as the national organ for publishing these mighty events, became itself a spiritualized and glorified object to an impassioned heart; and naturally, in the Oxford of that day, all hearts were awakened. There were, perhaps, of us gownsmen, two thousand *resident*[3] in Oxford, and dispersed through five-and-twenty colleges. In some of these the custom permitted the student to keep what are called 'short terms;' that is, the four terms of Michaelmas, Lent, Easter, and Act, were kept severally by a residence, in the aggregate, of ninety-one days, or thirteen weeks. Under this interrupted residence, accordingly, it was possible that a student might have a reason for going down to his home four times in the year. This made eight journeys to and fro. And as these homes lay dispersed through all the shires of the island, and most of us disdained all coaches except his majesty's mail, no city out of London could pretend to so extensive a connection with Mr. Palmer's establishment as Oxford. Naturally, therefore, it became a point of some interest with us, whose journeys revolved every six weeks on an average, to look a little into the executive details of the system. With some of these Mr. Palmer had no concern; they rested upon bye-laws not unreasonable, enacted by posting-houses for their own benefit, and upon others equally stern, enacted by the inside passengers for the illustration of their own exclusiveness.

These last were of a nature to rouse our scorn, from which the transition was not *very long* to mutiny. Up to this time, it had been the fixed assumption of the four inside people, (as an old tradition of all public carriages from the reign of Charles II.,) that they, the illustrious quaternion, constituted a porcelain variety of the human race, whose dignity would have been compromised by exchanging one word of civility with the three miserable delf ware outsides. Even to have kicked an outsider might have been held to attaint the foot concerned in that operation; so that, perhaps, it would have required an act of parliament to restore its purity of blood. What words, then, could express the horror, and the sense of treason, in that case, which *had* happened, where all three outsides, the trinity of Pariahs, made a vain attempt to sit down at the same breakfast table or dinner table with the consecrated four? I myself witnessed such an attempt; and on that occasion a benevolent old gentleman endeavored to soothe his three holy associates, by suggesting that, if the outsides were indicted for this criminal attempt at the next assizes, the court would regard it as a case of lunacy (or *delirium tremens*) rather than of treason. England owes much of her grandeur to the depth of the aristocratic element in her social composition. I am not the man to laugh at it. But sometimes it expressed itself in extravagant shapes. The course taken with the infatuated outsiders, in the particular attempt which I have noticed, was, that the waiter, beckoning them away from the privileged *salle-à-manger*, sang out, 'This way, my good men;' and then enticed them away off to the kitchen. But that plan had not always answered. Sometimes, though very rarely, cases occurred where the intruders, being stronger than usual, or more vicious than usual, resolutely refused to move, and so far carried their point, as to have a separate table arranged for themselves in a corner of the room. Yet, if an Indian screen could be found ample enough to plant them out from the very eyes of the high table, or *dais*, it then became possible to assume as a fiction of law — that the three delf fellows, after all, were not present. They could be ignored by the porcelain men, under the maxim, that objects not appearing, and not existing, are governed by the same logical construction.

Such now being, at that time, the usages of mail-coaches, what was to be done by us of young Oxford? We, the most aristocratic of people, who were addicted to the practice of looking down superciliously even upon the insides themselves as often very suspicious characters, were we voluntarily to court indignities? If our dress and bearing sheltered us, generally, from the suspicion of being 'raff,' (the name at that period for 'snobs,'[4]) we really *were* such constructively, by the place we assumed. If we did not submit to the deep shadow of eclipse, we entered at least the skirts of its penumbra. And the analogy of theatres was urged against us, where no man can complain of the annoyances incident to the pit or gallery, having his instant remedy in paying the higher price of the boxes. But the soundness of this analogy we disputed. In the case of the theatre, it cannot be pretended that the inferior situations have any separate attractions, unless the pit suits the purpose of the dramatic reporter. But the reporter or critic is a rarity. For most people, the sole benefit is in the price. Whereas, on the contrary, the outside of the mail had its own incommunicable advantages. These we could not forego. The higher price we should willingly have paid, but that was connected with the condition of riding inside, which was insufferable. The air, the freedom of prospect, the proximity to the horses, the elevation of seat — these were what we desired; but above all, the certain anticipation of purchasing occasional opportunities of driving.

Under coercion of this great practical difficulty, we instituted a searching inquiry into the true quality and valuation of the different apartments about the mail. We conducted this inquiry on metaphysical principles; and it was ascertained satisfactorily, that the roof of the coach, which some had affected to call the attics, and some the garrets, was really the drawing-room, and the box was the chief ottoman or sofa in that drawing-room; whilst it appeared that the inside, which had been traditionally regarded as the only room tenantable by gentlemen, was, in fact, the coal-cellar in disguise.

Great wits jump. The very same idea had not long before struck the celestial intellect of China. Amongst the presents carried out by our first embassy to that country was a state-coach. It had been specially selected as a personal gift by George III.; but the exact mode of using it was a mystery to Pekin. The ambassador, indeed, (Lord Macartney,) had made some dim and imperfect explanations upon the point; but as his excellency communicated these in a diplomatic whisper, at the very moment of his departure, the celestial mind was very feebly illuminated; and it became necessary to call a cabinet council on the grand state question — 'Where was the emperor to sit?' The hammer-cloth happened to be unusually gorgeous; and partly on that consideration, but partly also because the box offered the most elevated seat, and undeniably went foremost, it was resolved by acclamation that the box was the imperial place, and, *for the scoundrel who drove, he might sit where he could find a perch.* The horses, therefore, being harnessed, under a flourish of music and a salute of guns, solemnly his imperial majesty ascended his new English throne, having the first lord of the treasury on his right hand, and the chief jester on his left. Pekin gloried in the spectacle; and in the whole flowery people, constructively present by representation, there was but one discontented person, which was the coachman. This mutinous individual, looking as blackhearted as he really was, audaciously shouted, 'Where am *I* to sit?' But the privy council, incensed by his disloyalty, unanimously opened the door, and kicked him into the inside. He had all the inside places to himself; but such is the rapacity of ambition, that he was still dissatisfied. 'I say,' he cried out in an extempore petition, addressed to the emperor through the window, 'how am I to catch hold of the reins?' 'Any how,' was the answer; 'don't trouble *me*, man, in my glory; through the windows, through the key-holes — how you please.' Finally this contumacious coachman lengthened the checkstrings into a sort of jury-reins, communicating with the horses; with these he drove as steadily as may be supposed. The emperor returned after the briefest of circuits; he descended in great pomp from his throne, with the severest resolution never to remount it. A public thanksgiving was ordered for his majesty's prosperous escape from the disease of a broken neck; and the state-coach was dedicated for ever as a votive offering to the god Fo, Fo — whom the learned more accurately called Fi, Fi.

A revolution of this same Chinese character did young Oxford of that era effect in the constitution of mail-coach society. It was a perfect French revolution; and we had good reason to say, *Ca ira.* In fact, it soon became *too* popular. The 'public,' a well known character, particularly disagreeable, though slightly respectable, and notorious for affecting the chief seats in synagogues, had at first loudly opposed this revolution; but when the opposition showed itself to be ineffectual, our disagreeable friend went into it with headlong zeal. At first it was a sort of race between us; and, as the public is usually above thirty, (say generally from thirty to fifty years old,) naturally we of young Oxford, that averaged about twenty, had the advantage. Then the public took to bribing, giving fees to horse-keepers, &c., who hired out their persons as warming-pans on the box-seat. *That*, you know, was shocking to our moral sensibilities. Come to bribery, we observed, and there is an end to all morality, Aristotle's, Cicero's, or anybody's. And, besides, of what use was it? For *we* bribed also. And as our bribes to those of the public being demonstrated out of Euclid to be as five shillings to sixpence, here again young Oxford had the advantage. But the contest was ruinous to the principles of the stable establishment about the mails. The whole corporation was constantly bribed, rebribed, and often sur-rebribed; so that a horse-keeper, ostler, or helper, was held by the philosophical at that time to be the most corrupt character in the nation.

There was an impression upon the public mind, natural enough from the continually augmenting velocity of the mail, but quite erroneous, that an outside seat on this class of carriages was a post of danger. On the contrary, I maintained that, if a man had become nervous from some gipsy prediction in his childhood, allocating to a particular moon now approaching some unknown danger, and he should inquire earnestly, 'Whither can I go for shelter? Is a prison the safest retreat? Or a lunatic hospital? Or the British Museum?' I should have replied, 'Oh, no; I'll tell you what to do. Take lodgings for the next forty days on the box of his majesty's mail. Nobody can touch you there. If it is by bills at ninety days after date that you are made unhappy — if noters and protesters are the sort of wretches whose astrological shadows darken the house of life — then note you what I vehemently protest, viz., that no matter though the sheriff in every county should be running after you with his *posse*, touch a hair of your head he cannot whilst you keep house, and have your legal domicile on the box of the mail. It's felony to stop the mail; even the sheriff cannot do that. And an *extra* (no great matter if it grazes the sheriff) touch of the whip to the leaders at any time guarantees your safety.' In fact, a bedroom in a quiet house, seems a safe enough retreat; yet it is liable to its own notorious nuisances, to robbers by night, to rats, to fire. But the mail laughs at these terrors. To robbers, the answer is packed up and ready for delivery in the barrel of the guard's blunderbuss. Rats again! there *are* none about mail-coaches, any more than snakes in Van Troil's Iceland; except, indeed, now and then a parliamentary rat, who always hides his shame in the 'coal cellar.' And, as to fire, I never knew but one in a mail-coach, which was in the Exeter mail, and caused by an obstinate sailor bound to Davenport. Jack, making light of the law and the lawgiver that had set their faces against his offence, insisted on taking up a forbidden seat in the rear of the roof, from which he could exchange his own yarns with those of the guard. No greater offence was then known to mail-coaches; it was treason, it was *læsa majestas*, it was by tendency arson; and the ashes of Jack's pipe, falling amongst the straw of the hinder boot, containing the mail-bags, raised a flame which (aided by the wind of our motion) threatened a revolution in the republic of letters. But even this left the sanctity of the box unviolated. In dignified repose, the coachman and myself sat on, resting with benign composure upon our knowledge — that the fire would have to burn its way through four inside passengers before it could reach ourselves. With a quotation rather too trite, I remarked to the coachman, —

—— 'Jam proximus ardet
Ucalegon.'

But recollecting that the Virgilian part of his education might have been neglected, I interpreted so far as to say, that perhaps at that moment the flames were catching hold of our worthy brother and next-door neighbor Ucalegon. The coachman said nothing, but, by his faint sceptical smile, he seemed to be thinking that he knew better; for that in fact, Ucalegon, as it happened, was not in the way-bill.

No dignity is perfect which does not at some point ally itself with the indeterminate and mysterious. The connection of the mail with the state and the executive government — a connection obvious, but yet not strictly defined — gave to the whole mail establishment a grandeur and an official authority which did us service on the roads, and invested us with seasonable terrors. But perhaps these terrors were not the less impressive, because their exact legal limits were imperfectly ascertained. Look at those turnpike gates; with what deferential hurry, with what an obedient start, they fly open at our approach! Look at that long line of carts and carters ahead, audaciously usurping the very crest of the road. Ah! traitors, they do not hear us as yet; but as soon as the dreadful blast of our horn reaches them with the proclamation of our approach, see with what frenzy of trepidation they fly to their horses' heads, and deprecate our wrath by the precipitation of their crane-neck quarterings. Treason they feel to be their crime; each individual carter feels himself under the ban of confiscation and attainder: his blood is attainted through six generations, and nothing is wanting but the headsman and his axe, the block and the sawdust, to close up the vista of his horrors. What! shall it be within benefit of clergy to delay the king's message on the high road? — to interrupt the great respirations, ebb or flood, of the national intercourse — to endanger the safety of tidings, running day and night between all nations and languages? Or can it be fancied, amongst the weakest of men, that the bodies of the criminals will be given up to their widows for Christian burial? Now the doubts which were raised as to our powers did more to wrap them in terror, by wrapping them in uncertainty, than could have been effected by the sharpest definitions of the law from the Quarter Sessions. We, on our parts, (we, the collective mail, I mean,) did our utmost to exalt the idea of our privileges by the insolence with which we wielded them. Whether this insolence rested upon law that gave it a sanction, or upon conscious power, haughtily dispensing with that sanction, equally it spoke from a potential station; and the agent in each particular insolence of the moment, was viewed reverentially, as one having authority.

Sometimes after breakfast his majesty's mail would become frisky: and in its difficult wheelings amongst the intricacies of early markets, it would upset an apple cart, a cart loaded with eggs, &c. Huge was the affliction and dismay, awful was the smash, though, after all, I believe the damage might be levied upon the hundred. I, as far as possible, endeavored in such a case to represent the conscience and moral sensibilities of the mail; and, when wildernesses of eggs were lying poached under our horses' hoofs, then would I stretch forth my hands in sorrow, saying (in words too celebrated in those days from the false [5] echoes of Marengo) —'Ah! wherefore have we not time to weep over you?' which was quite impossible, for in fact we had not even time to laugh over them. Tied to post-office time, with an allowance in some cases of fifty minutes for eleven miles, could the royal mail pretend to undertake the offices of sympathy and condolence? Could it be expected to provide tears for the accidents of the road? If even it seemed to trample on humanity, it did so, I contended, in discharge of its own more peremptory duties.

Upholding the morality of the mail, *à fortiori* I upheld its rights, I stretched to the uttermost its privilege of imperial precedency, and astonished weak minds by the feudal powers which I hinted to be lurking constructively in the charters of this proud establishment. Once I remember being on the box of the Holyhead mail, between Shrewsbury and Oswestry, when a tawdry thing from Birmingham, some *Tallyho* or *Highflier*, all flaunting with green and gold, came up alongside of us. What a contrast to our royal simplicity of form and color is this plebeian wretch! The single ornament on our dark ground of chocolate color was the mighty shield of the imperial arms, but emblazoned in proportions as modest as a signet-ring bears to a seal of office. Even this was displayed only on a single panel, whispering, rather than proclaiming, our relations to the state; whilst the beast from Birmingham had as much writing and painting on its sprawling flanks as would have puzzled a decipherer from the tombs of Luxor. For some time this Birmingham machine ran along by our side — a piece of familiarity that seemed to us sufficiently jacobinical. But all at once a movement of the horses announced a desperate intention of leaving us behind. 'Do you see *that*?' I said to the coachman. 'I see,' was his short answer. He was awake, yet he waited longer than seemed prudent; for the horses of our audacious opponent had a disagreeable air of freshness and power. But his motive was loyal; his wish was that the Birmingham conceit should be full-blown before he froze it. When *that* seemed right, he unloosed, or, to speak by a stronger image, he sprang his known resources, he slipped our royal horses like cheetas, or hunting leopards, after the affrighted game. How they could retain such a reserve of fiery power after the work they had accomplished, seemed hard to explain. But on our side, besides the physical superiority, was a tower of strength, namely, the king's name, 'which they upon the adverse faction wanted.' Passing them without an effort, as it seemed, we threw them into the rear with so lengthening an interval between us, as proved in itself the bitterest mockery of their presumption; whilst our guard blew back a shattering blast of triumph, that was really too painfully full of derision.

I mention this little incident for its connection with what followed. A Welshman, sitting behind me, asked if I had not felt my heart burn within me during the continuance of the race? I said — no; because we were not racing with a mail, so that no glory could be gained. In fact, it was sufficiently mortifying that such a Birmingham thing should dare to challenge us. The Welshman replied, that he didn't see *that;* for that a cat might look at a king, and a Brummagem coach might lawfully race the Holyhead mail. '*Race* us perhaps,' I replied, 'though even *that* has an air of sedition, but not *beat* us. This would have been treason; and for its own sake I am glad that the Tallyho vas disappointed.' So dissatisfied did the Welshman seem with this opinion, that at last I was obliged to tell him a very fine story from one of our elder dramatists, viz. — that once, in some oriental region, when the prince of all the land, with his splendid court, were flying their falcons, a hawk suddenly flew at a majestic eagle; and in defiance of the eagle's prodigious advantages, in sight also of all the astonished field sportsmen, spectators, and followers, killed him on the spot. The prince was struck with amazement at the unequal contest, and with burning admiration for its unparalleled result. He commanded that the hawk should be brought before him; caressed the bird with enthusiasm, and ordered that, for the commemoration of his matchless courage, a crown of gold should be solemnly placed on the hawk's head; but then that, immediately after this coronation, the bird should be led off to execution, as the most valiant indeed of traitors, but not the less a traitor that had dared to rise in rebellion against his liege lord the eagle. 'Now,' said I to the Welshman, 'how painful it would have been to you and me as men of refined feelings, that this poor brute, the Tallyho, in the impossible case of a victory over us, should have been crowned with jewellery, gold, with Birmingham ware, or paste diamonds, and then led off to instant execution.' The Welshman doubted if that could be warranted by law. And when I hinted at the 10th of Edward III., chap. 15, for regulating the precedency of coaches, as being probably the statute relied on for the capital punishment of such offences, he replied drily — that if the attempt to pass a mail was really treasonable, it was a pity that the Tallyho appeared to have so imperfect an acquaintance with law.

These were among the gaieties of my earliest and boyish acquaintance with mails. But alike the gayest and the most terrific of my experiences rose again after years of slumber, armed with preternatural power to shake my dreaming sensibilities; sometimes, as in the slight case of Miss Fanny on the Bath road, (which I will immediately mention,) through some casual or capricious association with images originally gay, yet opening at some stage of evolution into sudden capacities of horror; sometimes through the more natural and fixed alliances with the sense of power so various lodged in the mail system.

The modern modes of travelling cannot compare with the mail-coach system in grandeur and power. They boast of more velocity, but not however as a consciousness, but as a fact of our lifeless knowledge, resting upon *alien* evidence; as, for instance, because somebody *says* that we have gone fifty miles in the hour, or upon the evidence of a result, as that actually we find ourselves in York four hours after leaving London. Apart from such an assertion, or such a result, I am little aware of the pace. But, seated on the old mail-coach, we needed no evidence out of ourselves to indicate the velocity. On this system the word was — *Non magna loquimur*, as upon railways, but *magna vivimus*. The vital experience of the glad animal sensibilities made doubts impossible on the question of our speed; we heard our speed, we saw it, we felt it as a thrilling; and this speed was not the product of blind insensate agencies, that had no sympathy to give, but was incarcerated in the fiery eyeballs of an animal, in his dilated nostril, spasmodic muscles, and echoing hoofs. This speed was incarnated in the *visible* contagion amongst brutes of some impulse, that, radiating into *their* natures, had yet its centre and beginning in man. The sensibility of the horse, uttering itself in the maniac light of his eye, might be the last vibration of such a movement; the glory of Salamanca might be the first — but the intervening link that connected them, that spread the earthquake of the battle into the eyeball of the horse, was the heart of man — kindling in the rapture of the fiery strife, and then propagating its own tumults by motions and gestures to the sympathies, more or less dim, in his servant the horse.

But now, on the new system of travelling, iron tubes and boilers have disconnected man's heart from the ministers of his locomotion. Nile nor Trafalgar has power any more to raise an extra bubble in a steam-kettle. The galvanic cycle is broken up for ever; man's imperial nature no longer sends itself forward through the electric sensibility of the horse; the inter-agencies are gone in the mode of communication between the horse and his master, out of which grew so many aspects of sublimity under accidents of mists that hid, or sudden blazes that revealed, of mobs that agitated, or midnight solitudes that awed. Tidings, fitted to convulse all nations, must henceforwards travel by culinary process; and the trumpet that once announced from afar the laurelled mail, heart-shaking, when heard screaming on the wind, and advancing through the darkness to every village or solitary house on its route, has now given way for ever to the pot-wallopings of the boiler.

Thus have perished multiform openings for sublime effects, for interesting personal communications, for revelations of impressive faces that could not have offered themselves amongst the hurried and fluctuating groups of a railway station. The gatherings of gazers about a mail-coach had one centre, and acknowledged only one interest. But the crowds attending at a railway station have as little unity as running water, and own as many centres as there are separate carriages in the train.

How else, for example, than as a constant watcher for the dawn, and for the London mail that in summer months entered about dawn into the lawny thickets of Marlborough Forest, couldst thou, sweet Fanny of the Bath road, have become known to myself? Yet Fanny, as the loveliest young woman for face and person that perhaps in my whole life I have beheld, merited the station which even *her* I could not willingly have spared; yet (thirty-five years later) she holds in my dreams; and though, by an accident of fanciful caprice, she brought along with her into those dreams a troop of dreadful creatures, fabulous and not fabulous, that were more abominable to a human heart than Fanny and the dawn were delightful.

Miss Fanny of the Bath road, strictly speaking, lived at a mile's distance from that road, but came so continually to meet the mail, that I on my frequent transits rarely missed her, and naturally connected her name with the great thoroughfare where I saw her; I do not exactly know, but I believe with some burthen of commissions to be executed in Bath, her own residence being probably the centre to which these commissions gathered. The mail coachman, who wore the royal livery, being one amongst the privileged few,[6] happened to be Fanny's grandfather. A good man he was, that loved his beautiful granddaughter; and, loving her wisely, was vigilant over her deportment in any case where young Oxford might happen to be concerned. Was I then vain enough to imagine that I myself, individually, could fall within the line of his terrors? Certainly not, as regarded any physical pretensions that I could plead; for Fanny (as a chance passenger from her own neighborhood once told me) counted in her train a hundred and ninety-nine professed admirers, if not open aspirants to her favor; and probably not one of the whole brigade but excelled myself in personal advantages. Ulysses even, with the unfair advantage of his accursed bow, could hardly have undertaken that amount of suitors. So the danger might have seemed slight — only that woman is universally aristocratic; it is amongst her nobilities of heart that she *is* so. Now, the aristocratic distinctions in my favor might easily with Miss Fanny have compensated my physical deficiencies. Did I then make love to Fanny? Why, yes; *mais oui donc;* as much love as one *can* make whilst the mail is changing horses, a process which ten years later did not occupy above eighty seconds; but *then*, viz., about Waterloo, it occupied five times eighty. Now, four hundred seconds offer a field quite ample enough for whispering into a young woman's ear a great deal of truth; and (by way of parenthesis) some trifle of falsehood. Grandpapa did right, therefore, to watch me. And yet, as happens too often to the grandpapas of earth, in a contest with the admirers of granddaughters, how vainly would he have watched me had I meditated any evil whispers to Fanny! She, it is my belief, would have protected herself against any man's evil suggestions. But he, as the result showed, could not have intercepted the opportunities for such suggestions. Yet he was still active; he was still blooming. Blooming he was as Fanny herself.

'Say, all our praises why should lords —'

No, that's not the line.

'Say, all our roses why should girls engross?'

The coachman showed rosy blossoms on his face deeper even than his granddaughter's, — *his* being drawn from the ale cask, Fanny's from youth and innocence, and from the fountains of the dawn. But, in spite of his blooming face, some infirmities he had; and one particularly (I am very sure no *more* than one,) in which he too much resembled a crocodile. This lay in a monstrous inaptitude for turning round. The crocodile, I presume, owes that inaptitude to the absurd *length* of his back; but in our grandpapa it arose rather from the absurd *breadth* of his back, combined, probably, with some growing stiffness in his legs. Now upon this crocodile infirmity of his I planted an easy opportunity for tendering my homage to Miss Fanny. In defiance of all his honorable vigilance, no sooner had he presented to us his mighty Jovian back (what a field for displaying to mankind his royal scarlet!) whilst inspecting professionally the buckles, the straps, and the silver turrets of his harness, than I raised Miss Fanny's hand to my lips, and, by the mixed tenderness and respectfulness of my manner, caused her easily to understand how happy it would have made me to rank upon her list as No. 10 or 12, in which case a few casualties amongst her lovers (and observe — they *hanged* liberally in those days) might have promoted me speedily to the top of the tree; as, on the other hand, with how much loyalty of submission I acquiesced in her allotment, supposing that she had seen reason to plant me in the very rearward of her favor, as No. 199+1. It must not be supposed that I allowed any trace of jest, or even of playfulness, to mingle with these expressions of my admiration; that would have been insulting to her, and would have been false as regarded my own feelings. In fact, the utter shadowyness of our relations to each other, even after our meetings through seven or eight years had been very numerous, but of necessity had been very brief, being entirely on mail-coach allowance — timed, in reality, by the General Post-Office — and watched by a crocodile belonging to the antepenultimate generation, left it easy for me to do a thing which few people ever *can* have done — viz., to make love for seven years, at the same time to be as sincere as ever creature was, and yet never to compromise myself by overtures that might have been foolish as regarded my own interests, or misleading as regarded hers. Most truly I loved this beautiful and ingenuous girl; and had it not been for the Bath and Bristol mail, heaven only knows what might have come of it. People talk of being over head and ears in love — now, the mail was the cause that I sank only over ears in love, which, you know, still left a trifle of brain to overlook the whole conduct of the affair. I have not mentioned the case at all for the sake of a dreadful result from it in after years of dreaming. But it seems, *ex abundanti*, to yield this moral — viz., that as, in England, the idiot and the half-wit are held to be under the guardianship of chancery, so the man making love, who is often but a variety of the same imbecile class, ought to be made a ward of the General Post-Office, whose severe course of *timing* and periodical interruption might intercept many a foolish declaration, such as lays a solid foundation for fifty years' repentance.

Ah, reader! when I look back upon those days, it seems to me that all things change or perish. Even thunder and lightning, it pains me to say, are not the thunder and lightning which I seem to remember about the time of Waterloo. Roses, I fear, are degenerating, and, without a Red revolution, must come to the dust. The Fannies of our island — though this I say with reluctance — are not improving; and the Bath road is notoriously superannuated. Mr. Waterton tells me that the crocodile does *not* change — that a cayman, in fact, or an alligator, is just as good for riding upon as he was in the time of the Pharaohs. *That* may be; but the reason is, that the crocodile does not live fast — he is a slow coach. I believe it is generally understood amongst naturalists, that the crocodile is a blockhead. It is my own impression that the Pharaohs were also blockheads. Now, as the Pharaohs and the crocodile domineered over Egyptian society, this accounts for a singular mistake that prevailed on the Nile. The crocodile made the ridiculous blunder of supposing man to be meant chiefly for his own eating. Man, taking a different view of the subject, naturally met that mistake by another; he viewed the crocodile as a thing sometimes to worship, but always to run away from. And this continued until Mr. Waterton changed the relations between the animals. The mode of escaping from the reptile he showed to be, not by running away, but by leaping on its back, booted and spurred. The two animals had misunderstood each other. The use of the crocodile has now been cleared up — it is to be ridden; and the use of man is, that he may improve the health of the crocodile by riding him a fox-hunting before breakfast. And it is pretty certain that any crocodile, who has been regularly hunted through the season, and is master of the weight he carries, will take a six-barred gate now as well as ever he would have done in the infancy of the pyramids.

Perhaps, therefore, the crocodile does *not* change, but all things else *do*: even the shadow of the pyramids grows less. And often the restoration in vision of Fanny and the Bath road, makes me too pathetically sensible of that truth. Out of the darkness, if I happen to call up the image of Fanny from thirty-five years back, arises suddenly a rose in June; or, if I think for an instant of the rose in June, up rises the heavenly face of Fanny. One after the other, like the antiphonies in the choral service, rises Fanny and the rose in June, then back again the rose in June and Fanny. Then come both together, as in a chorus; roses and Fannies, Fannies and roses, without end — thick as blossoms in paradise. Then comes a venerable crocodile, in a royal livery of scarlet and gold, or in a coat with sixteen capes; and the crocodile is driving four-in-hand from the box of the Bath mail. And suddenly we upon the mail are pulled up by a mighty dial, sculptured with the hours, and with the dreadful legend of TOO LATE. Then all at once we are arrived at Marlborough forest, amongst the lovely households[7] of the roe-deer: these retire into the dewy thickets; the thickets are rich with roses; the roses call up (as ever) the sweet countenance of Fanny, who, being the granddaughter of a crocodile, awakens a dreadful host of wild semi-legendary animals, — griffins, dragons, basilisks, sphinxes,— till at length the whole vision of fighting images crowds into one towering armorial shield, a vast emblazonry of human charities and human loveliness that have perished, but quartered heraldically with unutterable horrors of monstrous and demoniac natures, whilst over all rises, as a surmounting crest, one fair female hand, with the fore-finger pointing, in sweet, sorrowful admonition, upwards to heaven, and having power (which, without experience, I never could have believed) to awaken the pathos that kills in the very bosom of the horrors that madden the grief that gnaws at the heart, together with the monstrous creations of darkness that shock the belief, and make dizzy the reason of man. This is the peculiarity that I wish the reader to notice, as having first been made known to me for a possibility by this early vision of Fanny on the Bath road. The peculiarity consisted in the confluence of two different keys, though apparently repelling each other, into the music and governing principles of the same dream;

horror, such as possesses the maniac, and yet, by momentary transitions, grief, such as may be supposed to possess the dying mother when leaving her infant children to the mercies of the cruel. Unusually, and perhaps always, in an unshaken nervous system, these two modes of misery exclude each other — here first they met in horrid reconciliation. There was also a separate peculiarity in the quality of the horror. This was afterwards developed into far more revolting complexities of misery and incomprehensible darkness; and perhaps I am wrong in ascribing any value as a *causative* agency to this particular case on the Bath road — possibly it furnished merely an *occasion* that accidentally introduced a mode of horrors certain, at any rate, to have grown up, with or without the Bath road, from more advanced stages of the nervous derangement. Yet, as the cubs of tigers or leopards, when domesticated, have been observed to suffer a sudden development of their latent ferocity under too eager an appeal to their playfulness — the gaieties of sport in *them* being too closely connected with the fiery brightness of their murderous instincts — so I have remarked that the caprices, the gay arabesques, and the lovely floral luxuriations of dreams, betray a shocking tendency to pass into finer maniacal splendors. That gaiety, for instance, (for such at first it was,) in the dreaming faculty, by which one principal point of resemblance to a crocodile in the mail-coachman was soon made to clothe him with the form of a crocodile, and yet was blended with accessory circumstances derived from his *human* functions, passed rapidly into a further development, no longer gay or playful, but terrific, the most terrific that besieges dreams, viz.—the horrid inoculation upon each other of incompatible natures. This horror has always been secretly felt by man; it was felt even under pagan forms of religion, which offered a very feeble, and also a very limited gamut for giving expression to the human capacities of sublimity or of horror. We read it in the fearful composition of the sphinx. The dragon, again, is the snake inoculated upon the scorpion. The basilisk unites the mysterious malice of the evil eye, unintentional on the part of the unhappy agent, with the intentional venom of some other malignant natures. But these horrid complexities of evil agency are but *objectively* horrid; they inflict the horror suitable to their compound nature; but there is no insinuation that they *feel* that horror. Heraldry is so full of these fantastic creatures, that, in some zoologies, we find a separate chapter or a supplement dedicated to what is denominated heraldic zoology. And why not? For these hideous creatures, however visionary,[8] have a real traditionary ground in medieval belief—sincere and partly reasonable, though adulterating with mendacity, blundering, credulity, and intense superstition. But the dream-horror which I speak of, is far more frightful. The dreamer finds housed within himself—occupying, as it were, some separate chamber in his brain—holding, perhaps, from that station a secret and detestable commerce with his own heart—some horrid alien nature. What if it were his own nature repeated,—still, if the duality were distinctly perceptible, even *that*—even this mere numerical double of his own consciousness—might be a curse too mighty to be sustained. But how, if the alien nature contradicts his own, fights with it, perplexes, and confounds it? How, again, if not one alien nature, but two, but three, but four, but five, are introduced within what once he thought the inviolable sanctuary of himself? These, however, are horrors from the kingdoms of anarchy and darkness, which, by their very intensity, challenge the sanctity of concealment, and gloomily retire from exposition. Yet it was necessary to mention them, because the first introduction to such appearances (whether causal, or merely casual) lay in the heraldic monsters, (which monsters were themselves introduced though playfully,) by the transfigured coachman of the Bath mail.

GOING DOWN WITH VICTORY.

But the grandest chapter of our experience, within the whole mail-coach service, was on those occasions when we went down from London with the news of victory. A period of about ten years stretched from Trafalgar to Waterloo: the second and third years of which period (1806 and 1807) were comparatively sterile; but the rest, from 1805 to 1815 inclusively, furnished a long succession of victories; the least of which, in a contest of that portentous nature, had an inappreciable value of position — partly for its absolute interference with the plans of our enemy, but still more from its keeping alive in central Europe the sense of a deep-seated vulnerability in France. Even to tease the coasts of our enemy, to mortify them by continual blockades, to insult them by capturing if it were but a baubling schooner under the eyes of their arrogant armies, repeated from time to time a sullen proclamation of power lodged in a quarter to which the hopes of Christendom turned in secret. How much more loudly must this proclamation have spoken in the audacity[9] of having bearded the *elite* of their troops, and having beaten them in pitched battles! Five years of life it was worth paying down for the privilege of an outside place on a mail-coach, when carrying down the first tidings of any such event. And it is to be noted that, from our insular situation, and the multitude of our frigates disposable for the rapid transmission of intelligence, rarely did any unauthorized rumor steal away a prelibation from the aroma of the regular dispatches. The government official news was generally the first news.

From eight, P. M. to fifteen or twenty minutes later, imagine the mails assembled on parade in Lombard Street, where, at that time, was seated the General Post-Office. In what exact strength we mustered I do not remember; but, from the length of each separate *attelage*, we filled the street, though a long one, and though we were drawn up in double file. On *any* night the spectacle was beautiful. The absolute perfection of all the appointments about the carriages and the harness, and the magnificence of the horses, were what might first have fixed the attention. Every carriage, on every morning in the year, was taken down to an inspector for examination — wheels, axles, linchpins, pole, glasses, &c., were all critically probed and tested. Every part of every carriage had been cleaned, every horse had been groomed, with as much rigor as if they belonged to a private gentleman; and that part of the spectacle offered itself always. But the night before us is a night of victory; and, behold! to the ordinary display, what a heart-shaking addition! — horses, men, carriages — all are dressed in laurels and flowers, oak leaves and ribbons. The guards, who are his majesty's servants, and the coachmen, who are within the privilege of the post-office, wear the royal liveries of course; and as it is summer (for all the *land* victories were won in summer,) they wear, on this fine evening, these liveries exposed to view, without any covering of upper coats. Such a costume, and the elaborate arrangement of the laurels in their hats, dilated their hearts, by giving to them openly an *official* connection with the great news, in which already they have the general interest of patriotism. That great national sentiment surmounts and quells all sense of ordinary distinctions. Those passengers who happen to be gentlemen are now hardly to be distinguished as such except by dress. The usual reserve of their manner in speaking to the attendants has on this night melted away. One heart, one pride, one glory, connects every man by the transcendent bond of his English blood. The spectators, who are numerous beyond precedent, express their sympathy with these fervent feelings by continual hurrahs. Every moment are shouted aloud by the post-office servants the great ancestral names of cities known to history through a thousand years, — Lincoln, Winchester, Portsmouth, Gloucester, Oxford, Bristol, Manchester, York, Newcastle, Edinburgh, Perth, Glasgow, — expressing the grandeur of the empire by the antiquity of its towns, and the grandeur of the mail establishment by the diffusive radiation of its separate missions. Every moment you hear the thunder of lids locked down upon the mail-bags. That sound to each individual mail is the signal for drawing off, which process is the finest part of the entire spectacle. Then come the horses into play, — horses! can these be horses that (unless powerfully reined in) would bound off with the action and gestures of leopards? What stir! — what sea-like ferment! — what a thundering of wheels, what a trampling of horses! — what farewell cheers — what redoubling peals of brotherly congratulation, connecting the name of the particular mail — 'Liverpool for ever!' — with the name of the particular victory — 'Badajoz for ever!' or 'Salamanca for ever!' The half-slumbering consciousness that, all night long and all the next day — perhaps for even a longer period — many of these mails, like fire racing along a train of gunpowder, will be kindling at every instant new successions of burning joy, has an obscure effect of multiplying the victory itself, by multiplying to the imagination into infinity the stages of its progressive diffusion. A fiery arrow seems to be let loose, which from that moment is destined to travel, almost without intermission, westwards for three hundred [10] miles — northwards for six hundred; and the sympathy of our Lombard Street friends at parting is exalted a hundred fold by a sort of visionary sympathy with the approaching sympathies, yet unborn, which we are going to evoke.

Liberated from the embarrassments of the city, and issuing into the broad uncrowded avenues of the northern suburbs, we begin to enter upon our natural pace of ten miles an hour. In the broad light of the summer evening, the sun, perhaps, only just at the point of setting, we are seen from every story of every house. Heads of every age crowd to the windows — young and old understand the language of our victorious symbols — and rolling volleys of sympathizing cheers run along behind and before our course. The beggar, rearing himself against the wall, forgets his lameness — real or assumed — thinks not of his whining trade, but stands erect, with bold exulting smiles, as we pass him. The victory has healed him, and says — Be thou whole! Women and children, from garrets alike and cellars, look down or look up with loving eyes upon our gay ribbons and our martial laurels — sometimes kiss their hands, sometimes hang out, as signals of affection, pocket handkerchiefs, aprons, dusters, anything that lies ready to their hands. On the London side of Barnet, to which we draw near within a few minutes after nine, observe that private carriage which is approaching us. The weather being so warm, the glasses are all down; and one may read, as on the stage of a theatre, everything that goes on within the carriage. It contains three ladies, one likely to be 'mama,' and two of seventeen or eighteen, who are probably her daughters. What lovely animation, what beautiful unpremeditated pantomime, explaining to us every syllable that passes, in these ingenuous girls! By the sudden start and raising of the hands, on first discovering our laurelled equipage! — by the sudden movement and appeal to the elder lady from both of them — and by the heightened color on their animated countenances, we can almost hear them saying —

'See, see! Look at their laurels. Oh, mama! there has been a great battle in Spain; and it has been a great victory.' In a moment we are on the point of passing them. We passengers — I on the box, and the two on the roof behind me — raise our hats, the coachman makes his professional salute with the whip; the guard even, though punctilious on the matter of his dignity as an officer under the crown, touches his hat. The ladies move to us, in return, with a winning graciousness of gesture: all smile on each side in a way that nobody could misunderstand, and that nothing short of a grand national sympathy could so instantaneously prompt. Will these ladies say that we are nothing to *them?* Oh, no; they will not say *that.* They cannot deny — they do not deny — that for this night they are our sisters: gentle or simple, scholar or illiterate servant, for twelve hours to come — we on the outside have the honor to be their brothers. Those poor women again, who stop to gaze upon us with delight at the entrance of Barnet, and seem, by their air of weariness, to be returning from labor — do you mean to say that they are washerwomen and char-women? Oh, my poor friend, you are quite mistaken; they are nothing of the kind. I assure you they stand in a higher rank; for this one night they feel themselves by birthright to be daughters of England, and answer to no humbler title.

Every joy, however, even rapturous joy — such is the sad law of earth — may carry with it grief, or fear of grief, to some. Three miles beyond Barnet, we see approaching us another private carriage, nearly repeating the circumstances of the former case. Here, also, the glasses are all down — here, also, is an elderly lady seated; but the two amiable daughters are missing; for the single young person, sitting by the lady's side, seems to be an attendant — so I judge from her dress, and her air of respectful reserve. The lady is in mourning; and her countenance expresses sorrow. At first she does not look up; so that I believe she is not aware of our approach, until she hears the measured beating of our horses' hoofs. Then she raises her eyes to settle them painfully on our triumphal equipage. Our decorations explain the case to her at once; but she beholds them with apparent anxiety, or even with terror. Some time before this, I, finding it difficult to hit a flying mark, when embarrassed by the coachman's person and reins intervening, had given to the guard a *Courier* evening paper, containing the gazette, for the next carriage that might pass. Accordingly he tossed it in so folded that the huge capitals expressing some such legend as — GLORIOUS VICTORY, might catch the eye at once. To see the paper, however, at all, interpreted as it was by our ensigns of triumph, explained everything; and, if the guard were right in thinking the lady to have received it with a gesture of horror, it could not be doubtful that she had suffered some deep personal affliction in connection with this Spanish war.

Here now was the case of one, who, having formerly suffered, might, erroneously perhaps, be distressing herself with anticipations of another similar suffering. That same night, and hardly three hours later, occurred the reverse case. A poor woman, who too probably would find herself, in a day or two, to have suffered the heaviest of afflictions by the battle, blindly allowed herself to express an exultation so unmeasured in the news, and its details, as gave to her the appearance which amongst Celtic Highlanders is called *fey*. This was at some little town, I forget what, where we happened to change horses near midnight. Some fair or wake had kept the people up out of their beds. We saw many lights moving about as we drew near; and perhaps the most impressive scene on our route was our reception at this place. The flashing of torches and the beautiful radiance of blue lights (technically Bengal lights) upon the heads of our horses: the fine effect of such a showery and ghostly illumination falling upon flowers and glittering laurels, whilst all around the massy darkness seemed to invest us with walls of impenetrable blackness, together with the prodigious enthusiasm of the people, composed a picture at once scenical and affecting. As we staid for three or four minutes, I alighted. And immediately from a dismantled stall in the street, where perhaps she had been presiding at some part of the evening, advanced eagerly a middle-aged woman. The sight of my newspaper it was that had drawn her attention upon myself. The victory which we were carrying down to the provinces on *this* occasion was the imperfect one of Talavera. I told her the main outline of the battle. But her agitation, though not the agitation of fear, but of exultation rather, and enthusiasm, had been so conspicuous when listening, and when first applying for information, that I could not but ask her if she had not some relation in the Peninsular army. Oh! yes: her only son was there. In what regiment? He was a trooper in the 23d Dragoons. My heart sank within me as she made that answer. This sublime regiment, which an Englishman should never mention without raising his hat to their memory, had made the most memorable and effective charge recorded in military annals. They leaped their horses — *over* a trench where they could, *into* it, and with the result of death or mutilation when they could *not*. What proportion cleared the trench is nowhere stated. Those who *did*, closed up and went down upon the enemy with such divinity of fervor — (I use the word *divinity* by design: the inspiration of God must have prompted this movement to those whom even then he was calling to his presence) — that two results followed. As regarded the enemy, this 23d Dragoons, not, I believe, originally three hundred and fifty strong, paralyzed a French column, six thousand strong, then ascending the hill, and fixed the gaze of the whole French army. As regarded themselves, the 23d were supposed at first to have been all but annihilated; but eventually, I believe, not so many as one in four survived. And this, then, was the regiment — a regiment already for some hours known to myself and all London, as stretched, by a large majority, upon one bloody aceldama — in which the young trooper served whose mother was now talking with myself in a spirit of such hopeful enthusiasm. Did I tell her the truth? Had I the heart to break up her dreams? No. I said to myself, to-morrow, or the next day, she will hear the worst. For this night, wherefore should she not sleep in peace? After to-morrow, the chances are too many that peace will forsake her pillow. This brief respite, let her owe this to *my* gift and *my* forbearance. But, if I told her not of the bloody price that had been paid, there was no reason for suppressing the contributions from her son's regiment to the service and glory of the day. For the very few words that I had time for speaking, I governed myself accordingly. I showed her not the funeral banners under which the noble regiment was sleeping. I lifted not the overshadowing laurels from the bloody trench in which horse and rider lay mangled together. But I told her how these dear children of England, privates and officers, had leaped their horses over all obstacles as gaily as hunters to the morning's chase. I told her how they rode their horses into the mists of death, (saying to myself, but not saying to *her*,) and laid down their young lives for thee, O mother England! as willingly — poured out their noble blood as cheerfully — as ever, after a long day's sport, when infants, they had rested their wearied heads upon their mother's knees, or had sunk to sleep in her arms. It is singular that she seemed to have no fears, even after this knowledge that the 23d Dragoons had been conspicuously engaged, for her son's safety: but so much was she enraptured by the knowledge that *his* regiment, and therefore *he*, had rendered eminent service in the trying conflict — a service which had actually made them the foremost topic of conversation in London — that in the mere simplicity of her fervent nature, she threw her arms round my neck, and, poor woman, kissed me.

NOTES.

NOTE 1. Page 131.

Lady Madeline Gordon.

NOTE 2. Page 132.

'*Vast distances.*' — One case was familiar to mail-coach travellers, where two mails in opposite directions, north and south, starting at the same minute from points six hundred miles apart, met almost constantly at a particular bridge which exactly bisected the total distance.

NOTE 3. Page 133.

'*Resident.*' — The number on the books was far greater, many of whom kept up an intermitting communication with Oxford. But I speak of those only who were steadily pursuing their academic studies, and of those who resided constantly as *fellows*.

NOTE 4. Page 135.

'*Snobs,*' and its antithesis, '*nobs,*' arose among the internal fractions of shoemakers perhaps ten years later. Possibly enough, the terms may have existed much earlier; but they were then first made known, picturesquely and effectively, by a trial at some assizes which happened to fix the public attention.

NOTE 5. Page 142.

'*False echoes.*' — yes, false! for the words ascribed to Napoleon, as breathed to the memory of Desaix, never were uttered at all. They stand in the same category of theatrical inventions as the cry of the foundering *Vengeur*, as the vaunt of General Cambronne at Waterloo, '*La Garde meurt, mais ne se rend pas*,' as the repartees of Talleyrand.

NOTE 6. Page 149.

'*Privileged few.*' — The general impression was, that this splendid costume belonged of right to the mail-coachmen as their professional dress. But that was an error. To the guard it *did* belong, as a matter of course, and was essential as an official warrant, and a means of instant identification for his person, in the discharge of his important public duties. But the coachman, and especially if his place in the series did not connect him immediately with London and the General Post-Office, obtained the scarlet coat only as an honorary distinction after long or special service.

NOTE 7. Page 154.

'*Households.*' — Roe-deer do not congregate in herds like the fallow or the red deer, but by separate families, parents, and children; which feature of approximation to the sanctity of human hearths, added to their comparatively miniature and graceful proportions, conciliate to them an interest of a peculiarly tender character, if less dignified by the grandeurs of savage and forest life.

NOTE 8. Page 156.

'*However visionary.*' — But *are* they always visionary? the unicorn, the kraken, the sea-serpent, are all, perhaps, zoological facts. The unicorn, for instance, so far from being a lie, is rather *too* true; for, simply as a *monokeras*, he is found in the Himalaya, in Africa, and elsewhere, rather too often for the peace of what in Scotland would be called the *intending* traveller. That which really *is* a lie in the account of the unicorn — viz., his legendary rivalship with the lion — which lie may God preserve, in preserving the mighty imperial shield that embalms it — cannot be more destructive to the zoological pretensions of the unicorn, than are to the same pretensions in the lion our many popular crazes about his goodness and magnanimity, or the old fancy (adopted by Spenser, and noticed by so many among our elder poets) of his graciousness to maiden innocence. The wretch is the basest and most cowardly among the forest tribes ; nor has the sublime courage of the English bull-dog ever been so memorably exhibited as in his hopeless fight at Warwick with the cowardly and cruel lion called Wallace. Another of the traditional creatures, still doubtful, is the mermaid, upon which Southey once remarked to me, that, if it had been differently named (as, suppose, a mer-ape,) nobody would have questioned its existence any more than that of sea-cows, sea-lions, &c. The mermaid has been discredited by her human name and her legendary human habits. If she would not coquette so much with melancholy sailors, and brush her hair so assiduously upon solitary rocks, she would be carried on our books for as honest a reality, as decent a female, as many that are assessed to the poor-rates.

NOTE 9. Page 158.

'*Audacity!*' — Such the French accounted it ; and it has struck me that Soult would not have been so popular in London, at the period of her present Majesty's coronation, or in Manchester, on occasion of his visit to that town, if they had been aware of the insolence with which he spoke of us in notes written at intervals from the field of Waterloo. As though it had been mere felony in our army to look a French one in the face, he said more than once — 'Here are the English — we have them : they are caught *en flagrant delit*.' Yet no man should have known us better ; no man had drunk deeper from the cup of humiliation than Soult had in the north of Portugal, during the flight from an English army, and subsequently at Albuera, in the bloodiest of recorded battles.

NOTE 10. Page 160.

'*Three hundred.*' — Of necessity this scale of measurement, to an American, if he happens to be a thoughtless man, must sound ludicrous. Accordingly, I remember a case in which an American writer indulges himself in the luxury of a little lying, by ascribing to an Englishman a pompous account of the Thames, constructed entirely upon American ideas of grandeur, and concluding in something like these terms: — 'And, sir, arriving at London, this mighty father of rivers attains a breadth of at least two furlongs, having, in its winding course, traversed the astonishing distance of one hundred and seventy miles.' And this the candid American thinks it fair to contrast with the scale of the Mississippi. Now, it is hardly worth while to answer a pure falsehood gravely, else one might say that no Englishman out of Bedlam ever thought of looking in an island for the rivers of a continent; nor, consequently, could have thought of looking for the peculiar grandeur of the Thames in the length of its course, or in the extent of soil which it drains: yet, if he *had* been so absurd, the American might have recollected that a river, not to be compared with the Thames even as to volume of water — viz. the Tiber — has contrived to make itself heard of in this world for twenty-five centuries to an extent not reached, nor likely to be reached very soon, by any river, however corpulent, of his own land. The glory of the Thames is measured by the destiny of the population to which it ministers, by the commerce which it supports, by the grandeur of the empire in which, though far from the largest, it is the most influential stream. Upon some such scale, and not by a transfer of Columbian standards, is the course of our English mails to be valued. The American may fancy the effect of his own valuations to our English ears, by supposing the case of a Siberian glorifying his country in these terms: — 'These rascals, sir, in France and England, cannot march half a mile in any direction without finding a house where food can be had and lodging; whereas, such is the noble desolation of our magnificent country, that in many a direction for a thousand miles, I will engage a dog shall not find shelter from a snow-storm, nor a wren find an apology for breakfast.'

THE VISION OF SUDDEN DEATH.

[THE reader is to understand this present paper, in its two sections of *The Vision*, &c., and *The Dream-Fugue*, as connected with a previous paper on *The English Mail-Coach*. The ultimate object was the Dream-Fugue, as an attempt to wrestle with the utmost efforts of music in dealing with a colossal form of impassioned horror. The Vision of Sudden Death contains the mail-coach incident, which did really occur, and did really suggest the variations of the Dream, here taken up by the Fugue, as well as other variations not now recorded. Confluent with these impressions, from the terrific experience on the Manchester and Glasgow mail, were other and more general impressions, derived from long familiarity with the English mail, as developed in the former paper; impressions, for instance, of animal beauty and power, of rapid motion, at that time unprecedented, of connection with the government and public business of a great nation, but, above all, of connection with the national victories at an unexampled crisis,—the mail being the privileged organ for publishing and dispersing all news of that kind. From this function of the mail, arises naturally the introduction of

Waterloo into the fourth variation of the Fugue; for the mail itself having been carried into the dreams by the incident in the vision, naturally all the accessory circumstances of pomp and grandeur investing this national carriage followed in the train of the principal image.]

What is to be thought of sudden death? It is remarkable that, in different conditions of society it has been variously regarded as the consummation of an earthly career most fervently to be desired, and, on the other hand, as that consummation which is most of all to be deprecated. Cæsar the Dictator, at his last dinner party, (*cæna*,) and the very evening before his assassination, being questioned as to the mode of death which, in *his* opinion, might seem the most eligible, replied — 'That which should be most sudden.' On the other hand, the divine Litany of our English Church, when breathing forth supplications, as if in some representative character for the whole human race prostrate before God, places such a death in the very van of horrors. 'From lightning and tempest; from plague, pestilence, and famine; from battle and murder, and from sudden death, — *Good Lord, deliver us.*' Sudden death is here made to crown the climax in a grand ascent of calamities; it is the last of curses; and yet, by the noblest of Romans, it was treated as the first of blessings. In that difference, most readers will see little more than the difference between Christianity and Paganism. But there I hesitate. The Christian church may be right in its estimate of sudden death; and it is a natural feeling, though after all it may also be an infirm one, to wish for a quiet dismissal from life — as that which *seems* most reconcilable with meditation, with penitential retrospects, and with the humilities of farewell prayer. There does not, however, occur to me any direct scriptural warrant for this earnest petition of the English Litany. It seems rather a petition indulged to human infirmity, than exacted from human piety. And, however *that* may be, two remarks suggest themselves as prudent restraints upon a doctrine, which else *may* wander, and *has* wandered, into an uncharitable superstition. The first is this: that many people are likely to exaggerate the horror of a sudden death, (I mean the *objective* horror to him who contemplates such a death, not the *subjective* horror to him who suffers it,) from the false disposition to lay a stress upon words or acts, simply because by an accident they have become words or acts. If a man dies, for instance, by some sudden death when he happens to be intoxicated, such a death is falsely regarded with peculiar horror; as though the intoxication were suddenly exalted into a blasphemy. But *that* is unphilosophic. The man was, or he was not, *habitually* a drunkard. If not, if his intoxication were a solitary accident, there can be no reason at all for allowing special emphasis to this act, simply because through misfortune it became his final act. Nor, on the other hand, if it were no accident, but one of his *habitual* transgressions, will it be the more habitual or the more a transgression, because some sudden calamity, surprising him, has caused this habitual transgression to be also a final one? Could the man have had any reason even dimly to foresee his own sudden death, there would have been a new feature in his act of intemperance — a feature of presumption and irreverence, as in one that by possibility felt himself drawing near to the presence of God. But this is no part of the case supposed. And the only new element in the man's act is not any element of extra immorality, but simply of extra misfortune.

The other remark has reference to the meaning of the word *sudden*. And it is a strong illustration of the duty which for ever calls us to the stern valuation of words — that very possibly Cæsar and the Christian church do not differ in the way supposed; that is, do not differ by any difference of doctrine as between Pagan and Christian views of the moral temper appropriate to death, but that they are contemplating different cases. Both contemplate a violent death, a Βιαιοθανατος — death that is βιαιος: but the difference is — that the Roman by the word 'sudden' means an *unlingering* death: whereas the Christian Litany by 'sudden' means a death *without warning*, consequently without any available summons to religious preparation. The poor mutineer, who kneels down to gather into his heart the bullets from twelve firelocks of his pitying comrades, dies by a most sudden death in Cæsar's sense: one shock, one mighty spasm, one (possibly *not* one) groan, and all is over. But, in the sense of the Litany, his death is far from sudden; his offence, originally, his imprisonment, his trial, the interval between his sentence and its execution, having all furnished him with separate warnings of his fate — having all summoned him to meet it with solemn preparation.

Meantime, whatever may be thought of a sudden

death as a mere variety in the modes of dying, where death in some shape is inevitable — a question which, equally in the Roman and the Christian sense, will be variously answered according to each man's variety of temperament — certainly, upon one aspect of sudden death there can be no opening for doubt, that of all agonies incident to man it is the most frightful, that of all martyrdoms it is the most freezing to human sensibilities — namely, where it surprises a man under circumstances which offer (or which seem to offer) some hurried and inappreciable chance of evading it. Any effort, by which such an evasion can be accomplished, must be as sudden as the danger which it affronts. Even *that*, even the sickening necessity for hurrying in extremity where all hurry seems destined to be vain, self-baffled, and where the dreadful knell of *too* late is already sounding in the ears by anticipation — even that anguish is liable to a hideous exasperation in one particular case, namely, where the agonizing appeal is made not exclusively to the instinct of self-preservation, but to the conscience, on behalf of another life besides your own, accidentally cast upon *your* protection. To fail, to collapse in a service merely your own, might seem comparatively venial; though, in fact, it is far from venial. But to fail in a case where Providence has suddenly thrown into your hands the final interests of another — of a fellow-creature shuddering between the gates of life and death; this, to a man of apprehensive conscience, would mingle the misery of an atrocious criminality with the misery of a bloody calamity. The man is called upon, too probably, to die; but to die at the very moment when, by any momentary collapse, he is self-denounced as a murderer. He had but the twinkling of an eye for his effort, and that effort might, at the best, have been unavailing; but from this shadow of a chance, small or great, how if he has recoiled by a treasonable *lâcheté*? The effort *might* have been without hope; but to have risen to the level of that effort, would have rescued him, though not from dying, yet from dying as a traitor to his duties.

The situation here contemplated exposes a dreadful ulcer, lurking far down in the depths of human nature. It is not that men generally are summoned to face such awful trials. But potentially, and in shadowy outline, such a trial is moving subterraneously in perhaps all men's natures — muttering under ground in one world, to be realized perhaps in some other. Upon the secret mirror of our dreams such a trial is darkly projected at intervals, perhaps, to every one of us. That dream, so familiar to childhood, of meeting a lion, and, from languishing prostration in hope and vital energy, that constant sequel of lying down before him, publishes the secret frailty of human nature — reveals its deep-seated Pariah falsehood to itself — records its abysmal treachery. Perhaps not one of us escapes that dream; perhaps, as by some sorrowful doom of man, that dream repeats for every one of us, through every generation, the original temptation in Eden. Every one of us, in this dream, has a bait offered to the infirm places of his own individual will; once again a snare is made ready for leading him into captivity to a luxury of ruin; again, as in aboriginal Paradise, the man falls from innocence; once again, by infinite iteration, the ancient Earth groans to God, through her secret caves, over the weakness of her child; 'Nature, from her seat, sighing through all her works,' again 'gives signs of woe that all is lost;' and again the counter sigh is repeated to the sorrowing heavens of the endless rebellion against God. Many people think that one man, the patriarch of our race, could not in his single person execute this rebellion for all his race. Perhaps they are wrong. But, even if not, perhaps in the world of dreams every one of us ratifies for himself the original act. Our English right of 'Confirmation,' by which, in years of awakened reason, we take upon us the engagements contracted for us in our slumbering infancy, — how sublime a rite is that! The little postern gate, through which the baby in its cradle had been silently placed for a time within the glory of God's countenance, suddenly rises to the clouds as a triumphal arch, through which, with banners displayed and martial pomps, we make our second entry as crusading soldiers militant for God, by personal choice and by sacramental oath. Each man says in effect — 'Lo! I rebaptize myself; and that which once was sworn on my behalf, now I swear for myself.' Even so in dreams, perhaps, under some secret conflict of the midnight sleeper, lighted up to the consciousness at the time, but darkened to the memory as soon as all is finished, each several child of our mysterious race completes for himself the aboriginal fall.

As I drew near to the Manchester post-office, I found that it was considerably past midnight; but to my great relief, as it was important for me to be in Westmoreland by the morning, I saw by the huge saucer eyes of the mail, blazing through the gloom of overhanging houses, that my chance was not yet lost. Past the time it was; but by some luck, very unusual in my experience, the mail was not even yet ready to start. I ascended to my seat on the box, where my cloak was still lying as it had lain at the Bridgewater Arms. I had left it there in imitation of a nautical discoverer, who leaves a bit of bunting on the shore of his discovery, by way of warning off the ground the whole human race, and signalizing to the Christian and the heathen worlds, with his best compliments, that he has planted his throne for ever upon that virgin soil: henceforward claiming the *jus dominii* to the top of the atmosphere above it, and also the right of driving shafts to the centre of the earth below it; so that all people found after this warning, either aloft in the atmosphere, or in the shafts, or squatting on the soil, will be treated as trespassers — that is, decapitated by their very faithful and obedient servant, the owner of the said bunting. Possibly my cloak might not have been respected, and the *jus gentium* might have been cruelly violated in my person — for, in the dark, people commit deeds of darkness, gas being a great ally of morality — but it so happened that, on this night, there was no other outside passenger; and the crime, which else was but too probable, missed fire for want of a criminal. By the way, I may as well mention at this point, since a circumstantial accuracy is essential to the effect of my narrative, that there was no other person of any description whatever about the mail — the guard, the coachman, and myself being allowed for — except only one — a horrid creature of the class known to the world as insiders, but whom young Oxford called sometimes 'Trojans,' in opposition to our Grecian selves, and sometimes 'vermin.' A Turkish Effendi, who piques himself on good breeding, will never mention by name a pig. Yet it is but too often that he has reason to mention this animal; since constantly, in the streets of Stamboul, he has his trousers deranged or polluted by this vile creature running between his legs. But under any excess of hurry he is always careful, out of respect to the company he is dining with, to suppress the odious name, and to call the wretch 'that other creature,' as though all animal life beside formed one group, and this odious beast (to whom, as Chrysippus observed, salt serves as an apology for a soul) formed another and alien group on the outside of creation. Now I, who am an English Effendi, that think myself to understand good-breeding as well as any son of Othman, beg my reader's pardon for having mentioned an insider by his gross natural name. I shall do so no more: and, if I should have occasion to glance at so painful a subject, I shall always call him 'that other creature.' Let us hope, however, that no such distressing occasion will arise. But, by the way, an occasion arises at this moment; for the reader will be sure to ask, when we come to the story, 'Was this other creature present?' He was *not;* or more correctly, perhaps, *it* was not. We dropped the creature — or the creature, by natural imbecility dropped itself — within the first ten miles from Manchester. In the latter case, I wish to make a philosophic remark of a moral tendency. When I die, or when the reader dies, and by repute suppose of fever, it will never be known whether we died in reality of the fever or of the doctor. But this other creature, in the case of dropping out of the coach, will enjoy a coroner's inquest; consequently he will enjoy an epitaph. For I insist upon it, that the verdict of a coroner's jury makes the best of epitaphs. It is brief, so that the public all find time to read; it is pithy, so that the surviving friends (if any *can* survive such a loss) remember it without fatigue; it is upon oath, so that rascals and Dr. Johnsons cannot pick holes in it. 'Died through the visitation of intense stupidity, by impinging on a moonlight night against the off hind wheel of the Glasgow mail! Deodand upon the said wheel — two-pence.' What a simple lapidary inscription! Nobody much in the wrong but an off-wheel; and with few acquaintances; and if it were but rendered into choice Latin, though there would be a little bother in finding a Ciceronian word for 'off-wheel,' Marcellus himself, that great master of sepulchral eloquence, could not show a better. Why I call this little remark *moral*, is, from the compensation it points out. Here, by the supposition, is that other creature on the one side, the beast of the world; and he (or it) gets an epitaph. You and I, on the contrary, the pride of our friends, get none.

But why linger on the subject of vermin? Having mounted the box, I took a small quantity of laudanum, having already travelled two hundred and fifty miles — viz., from a point seventy miles beyond London, upon a simple breakfast. In the taking of laudanum there was nothing extraordinary. But by accident it drew upon me the special attention of my assessor on the box, the coachman. And in *that* there was nothing extraordinary. But by accident, and with great delight, it drew my attention to the fact that this coachman was a monster in point of size, and that he had but one eye. In fact he had been foretold by Virgil as —

'Monstrum horrendum, informe, ingens cui lumen ademptum.'

He answered in every point — a monster he was — dreadful, shapeless, huge, who had lost an eye. But why should *that* delight me? Had he been one of the Calendars in the Arabian Nights, and had paid down his eye as the price of his criminal curiosity, what right had *I* to exult in his misfortune? I did *not* exult: I delighted in no man's punishment, though it were even merited. But these personal distinctions identified in an instant an old friend of mine, whom I had known in the south for some years as the most masterly of mail-coachmen. He was the man in all Europe that could best have undertaken to drive six-in-hand full gallop over *Al Sirat* — that famous bridge of Mahomet across the bottomless gulf, backing himself against the Prophet and twenty such fellows. I used to call him *Cyclops mastigophorus*, Cyclops the whip-bearer, until I observed that his skill made whips useless, except to fetch off an impertinent fly from a leader's head; upon which I changed his Grecian name to Cyclops *diphrélates* (Cyclops the charioteer.) I, and others known to me, studied under him the diphrelatic art. Excuse, reader, a word too elegant to be pedantic. And also take this remark from me, as a *gage d'amitié* — that no word ever was or *can* be pedantic which, by supporting a distinction, supports the accuracy of logic; or which fills up a chasm for the understanding. As a pupil, though I paid extra fees, I cannot say that I stood high in his esteem. It showed his dogged honesty, (though, observe, not his discernment,) that he could not see my merits. Perhaps we ought to excuse his absurdity in this particular by remembering his want of an eye. *That* made him blind to my merits. Irritating as this blindness was, (surely it could not be envy!) he always courted my conversation, in which art I certainly had the whip-hand of him. On this occasion, great joy was at our meeting. But what was Cyclops doing here? Had the medical men recommended northern air, or how? I collected, from such explanations as he volunteered, that he had an interest at stake in a suit-at-law pending at Lancaster; so that probably he had got himself transferred to this station, for the purpose of connecting with his professional pursuits an instant readiness for the calls of his lawsuit.

Meantime, what are we stopping for? Surely, we've been waiting long enough. Oh, this procrastinating mail, and oh this procrastinating post-office! Can't they take a lesson upon that subject from *me*? Some people have called *me* procrastinating. Now you are witness, reader, that I was in time for *them*. But can *they* lay their hands on their hearts, and say that they were in time for me? I, during my life, have often had to wait for the post-office: the post-office never waited a minute for me. What are they about? The guard tells me that there is a large extra accumulation of foreign mails this night, owing to irregularities caused by war and by the packet service, when as yet nothing is done by steam. For an *extra* hour, it seems, the post-office has been engaged in threshing out the pure wheaten correspondence of Glasgow, and winnowing it from the chaff of all baser intermediate towns. We can hear the flails going at this moment. But at last all is finished. Sound your horn, guard. Manchester, good bye ; we've lost an hour by your criminal conduct at the post-office: which, however, though I do not mean to part with a serviceable ground of complaint, and one which really *is* such for the horses, to me secretly is an advantage, since it compels us to recover this last hour amongst the next eight or nine. Off we are at last, and at eleven miles an hour; and at first I detect no changes in the energy or in the skill of Cyclops.

From Manchester to Kendal, which virtually (though not in law) is the capital of Westmoreland, were at this time seven stages of eleven miles each. The first five of these, dated from Manchester, terminated in Lancaster, which was therefore fifty-five miles north of Manchester, and the same distance exactly from Liverpool. The first three terminated in Preston, (called, by way of distinction from other towns of that name, *proud* Preston,) at which place it was that the separate roads from Liverpool and from Manchester to the north became confluent. Within these first three stages lay the foundation, the progress, and termination of our night's adventure. During the first stage, I found out that Cyclops was mortal: he was liable to the shocking affection of sleep — a thing which I had never previously suspected. If a man is addicted to the vicious habit of sleeping, all the skill in aurigation of Apollo himself, with the horses of Aurora to execute the motions of his will, avail him nothing. 'Oh, Cyclops!' I exclaimed more than once, 'Cyclops, my friend; thou art mortal. Thou snorest.' Through this first eleven miles, however, he betrayed his infirmity — which I grieve to say he shared with the whole Pagan Pantheon — only by short stretches. On waking up, he made an apology for himself, which, instead of mending the matter, laid an ominous foundation for coming disasters. The summer assizes were now proceeding at Lancaster: in consequence of which, for three nights and three days, he had not lain down in a bed. During the day, he was waiting for his uncertain summons as a witness on the trial in which he was interested; or he was drinking with the other witnesses, under the vigilant surveillance of the attorneys. During the night, or that part of it when the least temptations existed to conviviality, he was driving. Throughout the second stage he grew more and more drowsy. In the second mile of the third stage, he surrendered himself finally and without a struggle to his perilous temptation. All his past resistance had but deepened the weight of this final oppression. Seven atmospheres of sleep seemed resting upon him; and to consummate the case, our worthy guard, after singing, 'Love amongst the Roses,' for the fiftieth or sixtieth time, without any invitation from Cyclops or myself, and without applause for his poor labors, had moodily resigned himself to slumber — not so deep doubtless as the coachman's, but deep enough for mischief; and having, probably, no similar excuse. And thus at last, about ten miles from Preston, I found myself left in charge of his Majesty's London and Glasgow mail, then running about eleven miles an hour.

What made this negligence less criminal than else

it must have been thought, was the condition of the roads at night during the assizes. At that time all the law business of populous Liverpool, and of populous Manchester, with its vast cincture of populous rural districts, was called up by ancient usage to the tribunal of Lilliputian Lancaster. To break up this old traditional usage required a conflict with powerful established interests, a large system of new arrangements, and a new parliamentary statute. As things were at present, twice in the year so vast a body of business rolled northwards, from the southern quarter of the county, that a fortnight at least occupied the severe exertions of two judges for its dispatch. The consequence of this was — that every horse available for such a service, along the whole line of road, was exhausted in carrying down the multitudes of people who were parties to the different suits. By sunset, therefore, it usually happened that, through utter exhaustion amongst men and horses, the roads were all silent. Except exhaustion in the vast adjacent county of York from a contested election, nothing like it was ordinarily witnessed in England.

On this occasion, the usual silence and solitude prevailed along the road. Not a hoof nor a wheel was to be heard. And to strengthen this false luxurious confidence in the noiseless roads, it happened also that the night was one of peculiar solemnity and peace. I myself, though slightly alive to the possibilities of peril, had so far yielded to the influence of the mighty calm as to sink into a profound reverie. The month was August, in which lay my own birth-day; a festival to every thoughtful man suggesting solemn and often sigh-born thoughts.[1] The county was my own native county — upon which, in its southern section, more than upon any equal area known to man past or present, had descended the original curse of labor in its heaviest form, not mastering the bodies of men only as of slaves, or criminals in mines, but working through the fiery will. Upon no equal space of earth, was, or ever had been, the same energy of human power put forth daily. At this particular season also of the assizes, that dreadful hurricane of flight and pursuit, as it might have seemed to a stranger, that swept to and from Lancaster all day long, hunting the county up and down, and regularly subsiding about sunset, united with the permanent distinction of Lancashire as the very metropolis and citadel of labor, to point the thoughts pathetically upon that counter vision of rest, of saintly repose from strife and sorrow, towards which, as to their secret haven, the profounder aspirations of man's heart are continually travelling. Obliquely we were nearing the sea upon our left, which also must, under the present circumstances, be repeating the general state of halcyon repose. The sea, the atmosphere, the light, bore an orchestral part in this universal lull. Moonlight, in the first timid tremblings of the dawn, were now blending: and the blendings were brought into a still more exquisite state of unity, by a slight silvery mist, motionless and dreamy, that covered the woods and fields, but with a veil of equable transparency. Except the feet of our own horses,

[1] 'Sigh-born:' I owe the suggestion of this word to an obscure remembrance of a beautiful phrase in Giraldus Gambrensis, viz., *suspiriosæ cogitationes*.

which, running on a sandy margin of the road, made little disturbance, there was no sound abroad. In the clouds, and on the earth, prevailed the same majestic peace; and in spite of all that the villain of a schoolmaster has done for the ruin of our sublimer thoughts, which are the thoughts of our infancy, we still believe in no such nonsense as a limited atmosphere. Whatever we may swear with our false feigning lips, in our faithful hearts we still believe, and must for ever believe, in fields of air traversing the total gulf between earth and the central heavens. Still, in the confidence of children that tread without fear *every* chamber in their father's house, and to whom no door is closed, we, in that Sabbatic vision which sometimes is revealed for an hour upon nights like this, ascend with easy steps from the sorrow-stricken fields of earth, upwards to the sandals of God.

Suddenly from thoughts like these, I was awakened to a sullen sound, as of some motion on the distant road. It stole upon the air for a moment; I listened in awe; but then it died away. Once roused, however, I could not but observe with alarm the quickened motion of our horses. Ten years' experience had made my eye learned in the valuing of motion; and I saw that we were now running thirteen miles an hour. I pretend to no presence of mind. On the contrary, my fear is, that I am miserably and shamefully deficient in that quality as regards action. The palsy of doubt and distraction hangs like some guilty weight of dark unfathomed remembrances upon my energies, when the signal is flying for *action*. But, on the other hand, this accursed gift I have, as regards *thought*, that in the first step towards the possibility of a misfortune, I see its total evolution: in the radix I see too certainly and too instantly its entire expansion; in the first syllable of the dreadful sentence, I read already the last. It was not that I feared for ourselves. What could injure *us*? Our bulk and impetus charmed us against peril in any collision. And I had rode through too many hundreds of perils that were frightful to approach, that were matter of laughter as we looked back upon them, for any anxiety to rest upon *our* interests. The mail was not built, I felt assured, nor bespoke, that could betray *me* who trusted to its protection. But any carriage that we could meet would be frail and light in comparison of ourselves. And I remarked this ominous accident of our situation. We were on the wrong side of the road. But then the other party, if other there was, might also be on the wrong side; and two wrongs might make a right. *That* was not likely. The same motive which had drawn *us* to the right-hand side of the road, viz., the soft beaten sand, as contrasted with the paved centre, would prove attractive to others. Our lamps, still lighted, would give the impression of vigilance on our part. And every creature that met us, would rely upon *us* for quartering.[1] All this, and if the separate links of the anticipation had been a thousand times more, I saw — not discursively or by effort — but as by one flash of horrid intuition.

Under this steady though rapid anticipation of the

[1] '*Quartering*' — this is the technical word, and, I presume, derived from the French *cartayer*, to evade a rut or any obstacle.

evil which *might* be gathering ahead, ah, reader! what a sullen mystery of fear, what a sigh of woe, seemed to steal upon the air, as again the far-off sound of a wheel was heard! A whisper it was — a whisper from, perhaps, four miles off — secretly announcing a ruin that, being foreseen, was not the less inevitable. What could be done — who was it that could do it — to check the storm-flight of these maniacal horses? What! could I not seize the reins from the grasp of the slumbering coachman? You, reader, think that it would have been in *your* power to do so. And I quarrel not with your estimate of yourself. But, from the way in which the coachman's hand was viced between his upper and lower thigh, this was impossible. The guard subsequently found it impossible, after this danger had passed. Not the grasp only, but also the position of this Polyphemus, made the attempt impossible. You still think otherwise. See, then, that bronze equestrian statue. The cruel rider has kept the bit in his horse's mouth for two centuries. Unbridle him, for a minute, if you please, and wash his mouth with water. Or stay, reader, unhorse me that marble emperor: knock me those marble feet from those marble stirrups of Charlemagne.

The sounds ahead strengthened, and were now too clearly the sounds of wheels. Who and what could it be? Was it industry in a taxed cart? Was it youthful gaiety in a gig? Whoever it was, something must be attempted to warn them. Upon the other party rests the active responsibility, but upon *us* — and, woe is me! that *us* was my single self — rest the responsibility of warning. Yet, how should this be accomplished? Might I not seize the guard's horn? Already, on the first thought, I was making my way over the roof to the guard's seat. But this, from the foreign mail's being piled upon the roof, was a difficult, and even dangerous attempt, to one cramped by nearly three hundred miles of outside travelling. And, fortunately, before I had lost much time in the attempt, our frantic horses swept round an angle of the road, which opened upon us the stage where the collision must be accomplished, the parties that seemed summoned to the trial, and the impossibility of saving them by any communication with the guard.

Before us lay an avenue, straight as an arrow, six hundred yards, perhaps, in length; and the umbrageous trees, which rose in a regular line from either side, meeting high overhead, gave to it the character of a cathedral aisle. These trees lent a deeper solemnity to the early light; but there was still light enough to perceive, at the further end of this gothic aisle, a light, reedy gig, in which were seated a young man, and, by his side, a young lady. Ah, young sir! what are you about? If it is necessary that you should whisper your communications to this young lady — though really I see nobody at this hour, and on this solitary road, likely to overhear your conversation — is it, therefore, necessary that you should carry your lips forward to hers? The little carriage is creeping on at one mile an hour; and the parties within it, being thus tenderly engaged, are naturally bending down their heads. Between them and eternity, to all human calculation, there is but a minute and a half. What is it that I shall do? Strange it is, and to a mere auditor of the tale, might seem laughable, that I should need a suggestion from the *Iliad* to prompt the sole recourse that remained. But so it was. Suddenly I remembered the shout of Achilles, and its effect. But could I pretend to shout like the son of Peleus, aided by Pallas? No, certainly: but then I needed not the shout that should alarm all Asia militant; a shout would suffice, such as should carry terror into the hearts of two thoughtless young people, and one gig horse. I shouted — and the young man heard me not. A second time I shouted — and now he heard me, for now he raised his head.

Here, then, all had been done that, by me, *could* be done: more on *my* part was not possible. Mine had been the first step: the second was for the young man: the third was for God. If, said I, the stranger is a brave man, and if, indeed, he loves the young girl at his side — or, loving her not, if he feels the obligation pressing upon every man worthy to be called a man, of doing his utmost for a woman confided to his protection — he will at least make some effort to save her. If *that* fails, he will not perish the more, or by a death more cruel, for having made it; and he will die as a brave man should, with his face to the danger, and with his arm about the woman that he sought in vain to save. But if he makes no effort, shrinking, without a struggle, from his duty, he himself will not the less certainly perish for this baseness of poltroonery. He will die no less: and why not? Wherefore should we grieve that there is one craven less in the world? No; *let* him perish, without a pitying thought of ours wasted upon him; and, in that case, all our grief will be reserved for the fate of the helpless girl, who now, upon the least shadow of failure in *him*, must, by the fiercest of translations — must, without time for a prayer — must, within seventy seconds, stand before the judgment-seat of God.

But craven he was not: sudden had been the call upon him, and sudden was his answer to the call. He saw, he heard, he comprehended, the ruin that was coming down: already its gloomy shadow darkened above him; and already he was measuring his strength to deal with it. Ah! what a vulgar thing does courage seem, when we see nations buying it and selling it for a shilling a day: ah! what a sublime thing does courage seem, when some fearful crisis on the great deeps of life carries a man, as if running before a hurricane, up to the giddy crest of some mountainous wave, from which accordingly as he chooses his course, he describes two courses, and a voice says to him audibly, 'This way lies hope; take the other way and mourn for ever!' Yet, even then, amidst the raving of the seas and the frenzy of the danger, the man is able to confront his situation — is able to retire for a moment into solitude with God, and to seek all his counsel from *him!* For seven seconds, it might be, of his seventy, the stranger settled his countenance steadfastly upon us, as if to search and value every element in the conflict before him. For five seconds more he sate immovably, like one that mused on some great purpose. For five he sate with eyes upraised, like one that prayed in sorrow, under some extremity of doubt, for wisdom to guide him towards the better choice. Then suddenly he rose; stood upright; and, by a sudden strain upon the reins, raising his horse's forefeet from the ground, he slewed him round on the pivot of his hind legs, so as to plant the little equipage in a position nearly at right angles to ours. Thus far his condition was not improved; except as a first step had been taken towards the possibility of a second. If no more were done, nothing was done; for the little carriage still occupied the very centre of our path, though in an altered direction. Yet even now it may not be too late: fifteen of the twenty seconds may still be unexhausted; and one almighty bound forward may avail to clear the ground. Hurry then, hurry! for the flying moments — *they* hurry! Oh hurry, hurry, my brave young man! for the cruel hoofs of our horses — *they* also hurry! Fast are the flying moments, faster are the hoofs of our horses. Fear not for *him*, if human energy can suffice: faithful was he that drove, to his terrific duty; faithful was the horse to *his* command. One blow, one impulse given with voice and hand by the stranger, one rush from the horse, one bound as if in the act of rising to a fence, landed the docile creature's forefeet upon the crown or arching centre of the road. The larger half of the little equipage had then cleared our over-towering shadow: *that* was evident even to my own agitated sight. But it mattered little that one wreck should float off in safety, if upon the wreck that perished were embarked the human freightage. The rear part of the carriage — was *that* certainly beyond the line of absolute ruin? What power could answer the question? Glance of eye, thought of man, wing of angel, which of these had speed enough to sweep between the question and the answer, and divide the one from the other? Light does not tread upon the steps of light more indivisibly, than did our all-conquering arrival upon the escaping efforts of the gig. *That* must the young man have felt too plainly. His back was now turned to us; not by sight could he any longer communicate with the peril; but by the dreadful rattle of our harness, too truly had his ear been instructed — that all was finished as regarded any further effort of *his*. Already in resignation he had rested from his struggle; and perhaps, in his heart he was whispering — 'Father, which art above, do thou finish in heaven what I on earth have attempted.' We ran past them faster than ever mill-race in our inexorable flight. Oh, raving of hurricanes that must have sounded in their young ears at the moment of our transit! Either with the swingle-bar, or with the haunch of our near leader, we had struck the off-wheel of the little gig, which stood rather obliquely and not quite so far advanced as to be accurately parallel with the near wheel. The blow, from the fury of our passage, resounded terrifically. I rose in horror, to look upon the ruins we might have caused. From my elevated station I looked down, and looked back upon the scene, which in a moment told its tale, and wrote all its records on my heart for ever.

The horse was planted immovably, with his fore-feet upon the paved crest of the central road. He of the whole party was alone untouched by the passion of death. The little cany carriage — partly perhaps from the dreadful torsion of the wheels in its recent movement, partly from the thundering blow we had given to it — as if it sympathized with human horror, was all alive with tremblings and shiverings. The young man sat like a rock. He stirred not at all. But *his* was the steadiness of agitation frozen into rest by horror. As yet he dared not to look round; for he knew that, if anything remained to do, by him it could no longer be done. And as yet he knew not for certain if their safety were accomplished. But the lady ——

But the lady ——! Oh heavens! will that spectacle ever depart from my dreams, as she rose and sank upon her seat, sank and rose, threw up her arms wildly to heaven, clutched at some visionary object in the air, fainting, praying, raving, despairing! Figure to yourself, reader, the elements of the case; suffer me to recall before your mind the circumstances of the unparalleled situation. From the silence and deep peace of this saintly summer night — from the pathetic blending of this sweet moonlight, dawnlight, dreamlight — from the manly tenderness of this flattering, whispering, murmuring love — suddenly as from the woods and fields — suddenly as from the chambers of the air opening in revelation — suddenly as from the ground yawning at her feet, leaped upon her, with the flashing of cataracts, Death the crownèd phantom, with all the equipage of his terrors, and the tiger roar of his voice.

The moments were numbered. In the twinkling of an eye our flying horses had carried us to the termination of the umbrageous aisle; at right angles we wheeled into our former direction; the turn of the road carried the scene out of my eyes in an instant, and swept it into my dreams for ever.

DREAM-FUGUE.

ON THE ABOVE THEME OF SUDDEN DEATH.

'Whence the sound
Of instruments, that made melodious chime,
Was heard, of harp and organ; and who mov'd
Their stops and chords, was seen; his volant touch
Instinct through all proportions, low and high,
Fled and pursued transverse the resonant fugue.'

Par. Lost, B. XI.

Tumultuosissimamente.

Passion of Sudden Death! that once in youth I read and interpreted by the shadows of thy averted[1] signs! — Rapture of panic taking the shape which amongst tombs in churches I have seen, of woman bursting her sepulchral bonds — of woman's Ionic form bending forward from the ruins of her grave with arching foot, with eyes upraised, with clasped adoring hands — waiting, watching, trembling, praying, for the trumpet's call to rise from dust for ever! — Ah, vision too fearful of shuddering humanity on the brink of abysses! vision that didst start back — that didst reel away — like a shrivelling scroll from before the wrath of fire racing on the wings of the wind! Epilepsy so brief of horror — wherefore is it that thou canst not die? Passing so suddenly into darkness, wherefore is it that still thou sheddest thy sad funeral blights upon the gorgeous mosaics of dreams? Fragment of music too stern, heard once and heard no more, what aileth thee that

[1] '*Averted* signs.' — I read the course and changes of the lady's agony in the succession of her involuntary gestures; but let it be remembered that I read all this from the rear, never once catching the lady's full face, and even her profile imperfectly.

thy deep rolling chords come up at intervals through all the worlds of sleep, and after thirty years have lost no element of horror?

1.

Lo, it is summer, almighty summer! The everlasting gates of life and summer are thrown open wide; and on the ocean, tranquil and verdant as a savanna, the unknown lady from the dreadful vision and I myself are floating: she upon a fairy pinnace, and I upon an English three-decker. But both of us are wooing gales of festal happiness within the domain of our common country — within that ancient watery park — within that pathless chase where England takes her pleasure as a huntress through winter and summer, and which stretches from the rising to the setting sun. Ah! what a wilderness of floral beauty was hidden, or was suddenly revealed, upon the tropic islands, through which the pinnace moved. And upon her deck what a bevy of human flowers — young women how lovely, young men how noble, that were dancing together, and slowly drifting towards *us* amidst music and incense, amidst blossoms from forests and gorgeous corymbi from vintages, amidst natural carolling and the echoes of sweet girlish laughter. Slowly the pinnace nears us, gaily she hails us, and slowly she disappears beneath the shadow of our mighty bows. But then, as at some signal from heaven, the music and the carols, and the sweet echoing of girlish laughter — all are hushed. What evil has smitten the pinnace, meeting or overtaken her? Did ruin to our friends couch within our own dreadful shadow? Was our shadow the shadow of death? I looked over the bow for an answer; and, behold! the pinnace was dismantled; the revel and the revellers were found no more; the glory of the vintage was dust; and the forest was left without a witness to its beauty upon the seas. 'But where,' and I turned to our own crew—'Where are the lovely women that danced beneath the awning of flowers and clustering corymbi? Whither have fled the noble young men that danced with *them*?' Answer there was none. But suddenly the man at the mast-head, whose countenance darkened with alarm, cried out—'Sail on the weather beam! Down she comes upon us: in seventy seconds she will founder.'

2.

I looked to the weather side, and the summer had departed. The sea was rocking, and shaken with gathering wrath. Upon its surface sate mighty mists, which grouped themselves into arches and long cathedral aisles. Down one of these, with the fiery pace of a quarrel from a cross-bow, ran a frigate right athwart our course. 'Are they mad?' some voice exclaimed from our deck. 'Are they blind? Do they woo their ruin?' But in a moment, as she was close upon us, some impulse of a heady current or sudden vortex gave a wheeling bias to her course, and off she forged without a shock. As she ran past us, high aloft amongst the shrouds stood the lady of the pinnace. The deeps opened ahead in malice to receive her, towering surges of foam ran after her, the billows were fierce to catch her. But far away she was borne into desert spaces of the sea: whilst still by sight I followed her, as she ran before the howling gale, chased by angry sea-birds and by maddening billows; still I saw her, as at the moment when she ran past us, amongst the shrouds, with her white draperies streaming before the wind. There she stood with hair dishevelled, one hand clutched amongst the tackling — rising, sinking, fluttering, trembling, praying — there for leagues I saw her as she stood, raising at intervals one hand to heaven, amidst the fiery crests of the pursuing waves and the raving of the storm; until at last, upon a sound from afar of malicious laughter and mockery, all was hidden for ever in driving showers; and afterwards, but when I know not, and how I know not.

3.

Sweet funeral bells from some incalculable distance, wailing over the dead that die before the dawn, awakened me as I slept in a boat moored to some familiar shore. The morning twilight even then was breaking; and, by the dusky revelations which it spread, I saw a girl adorned with a garland of white roses about her head for some great festival, running along the solitary strand with extremity of haste. Her running was the running of panic; and often she looked back as to some dreadful enemy in the rear. But when I leaped ashore, and followed on her steps to warn her of a peril in front, alas! from me she fled as from another peril; and vainly I shouted to her of quicksands that lay ahead. Faster and faster she ran; round a promontory of rocks she wheeled out of sight; in an instant I also wheeled round it, but only to see the treacherous sands gathering above her head. Already her person was buried; only the fair young head and the diadem of white roses around it were still visible to the pitying heavens; and, last of all, was visible one marble arm. I saw by the early twilight this fair young head, as it was sinking down to darkness — saw this marble arm, as it rose above her head and her treacherous grave, tossing, faultering, rising, clutching as at some false deceiving hand stretched out from the clouds — saw this marble arm uttering her dying hope, and then her dying despair. The head, the diadem, the arm, — these all had sunk; at last over these also the cruel quicksand had closed; and no memorial of the fair young girl remained on earth, except my own solitary tears, and the funeral bells from the desert seas, that, rising again more softly, sang a requiem over the grave of the buried child, and over her blighted dawn.

I sate, and wept in secret the tears that men have ever given to the memory of those that died before the dawn, and by the treachery of earth, our mother. But the tears and funeral bells were hushed suddenly by a shout as of many nations, and by a roar as from some great king's artillery advancing rapidly along the valleys, and heard afar by its echoes among the mountains. 'Hush!' I said, as I bent my ear earthwards to listen — 'hush! — this either is the very anarchy of strife, or else' — and then I listened more profoundly, and said as I raised my head — 'or else, oh heavens! it is *victory* that swallows up all strife.'

4.

Immediately, in trance, I was carried over land and sea to some distant kingdom, and placed upon a triumphal car, amongst companions crowned with laurel. The darkness of gathering midnight, brooding over all the land, hid from us the mighty crowds that were weaving restlessly about our carriage as a centre — we heard them, but we saw them not. Tidings had arrived, within an hour, of a grandeur that measured itself against centuries; too full of pathos they were, too full of joy that acknowledged no fountain but God, to utter themselves by other language than by tears, by restless anthems, by reverberations rising from every choir, of the *Gloria in excelsis.* These tidings we that sate upon the laurelled car had it for our privilege to publish amongst all nations. And already, by signs audible through the darkness, by snortings and tramplings, our angry horses, that knew no fear of fleshly weariness, upbraided us with delay. Wherefore *was* it that we delayed? We waited for a secret word, that should bear witness to the hope of nations, as now accomplished for ever. At midnight the secret word arrived; which word was — Waterloo and Recovered Christendom! The dreadful word shone by its own light; before us it went; high above our leaders' heads it rode and spread a golden light over the paths which we traversed. Every city, at the presence of the secret word, threw open its gates to receive us. The rivers were silent as we crossed. All the infinite forests, as we ran along their margins, shivered in homage to the secret word. And the darkness comprehended it.

Two hours after midnight we reached a mighty minster. Its gates, which rose to the clouds, were closed. But when the dreadful word, that rode before us, reached them with its golden light, silently they moved back upon their hinges; and at a flying gallop our equipage entered the grand aisle of the cathedral. Headlong was our pace; and at every altar, in the little chapels and oratories to the right hand and left of our course, the lamps, dying or sickening, kindled anew in sympathy with the secret word that was flying past. Forty leagues we might have run in the cathedral, and as yet no strength of morning light had reached us, when we saw before us the aërial galleries of the organ and the choir. Every pinnacle of the fretwork, every station of advantage amongst the traceries, was crested by white-robed choristers, that sang deliverance; that wept no more tears, as once their fathers had wept; but at intervals that sang together to the generations, saying —

'Chaunt the deliverer's praise in every tongue,'

and receiving answers from afar,

—— 'such as once in heaven and earth were sung.'

And of their chaunting was no end; of our headlong pace was neither pause nor remission.

Thus, as we ran like torrents — thus, as we swept with bridal rapture over the Campo Santo[1] of the cathedral graves — suddenly we became aware of a vast

---

[1] *Campo Santo.* — It is probable that most of my readers will be acquainted with the history of the Campo Santo at Pisa — composed of earth brought from Jerusalem for a bed of sanctity, as the highest prize which the noble piety of crusaders could ask or imagine. There is another Campo Santo at Naples, formed, however, (I presume,) on the example given by Pisa. Possibly the idea may have been more extensively copied. To readers who are unacquainted with England, or who (being

necropolis rising upon the far-off horizon — a city of sepulchres, built within the saintly cathedral for the warrior dead that rested from their feuds on earth. Of purple granite was the necropolis; yet, in the first minute, it lay like a purple stain upon the horizon — so mighty was the distance. In the second minute it trembled through many changes, growing into terraces and towers of wondrous altitude, so mighty was the pace. In the third minute already, with our dreadful gallop, we were entering its suburbs. Vast sarcophagi rose on every side, having towers and turrets that, upon the limits of the central aisle, strode forward with haughty intrusion, that ran back with mighty shadows into answering recesses. Every sarcophagus showed many bas-reliefs, — bas-reliefs of battles — bas-reliefs of battle-fields; of battles from forgotten ages — of battles from yesterday — of battle-fields that, long since, nature had healed and reconciled to herself with the sweet oblivion of flowers — of battle-fields that were yet angry and crimson with carnage. Where the terraces ran, there did *we* run; where the towers curved, there did *we* curve. With the flight of swallows our horses swept round every angle. Like rivers in flood, wheeling round headlands; like hurricanes that side into the secrets of forests; faster than ever light unwove the mazes of darkness, our flying equipage carried

English) are yet unacqainted with the cathedral cities of England, it may be right to mention that the graves within-side the cathedrals often form a flat pavement over which carriages and horses might roll; and perhaps a boyish remembrance of one particular cathedral, across which I had seen passengers walk and burdens carried, may have assisted my dream.

earthly passions — kindled warrior instincts — amongst the dust that lay around us; dust oftentimes of our noble fathers that had slept in God from Créci to Trafalgar. And now had we reached the last sarcophagus, now were we abreast of the last bas-relief, already had we recovered the arrow-like flight of the illimitable central aisle, when coming up this aisle to meet us we beheld a female infant that rode in a carriage as frail as flowers. The mists, which went before her, hid the fawns that drew her, but could not hide the shells and tropic flowers with which she played — but could not hide the lovely smiles by which she uttered her trust in the mighty cathedral, and in the cherubim that looked down upon her from the topmost shafts of its pillars. Face to face she was meeting us; face to face she rode, as if danger there were none. 'Oh, baby!' I exclaimed, 'shalt thou be the ransom for Waterloo? Must we, that carry tidings of great joy to every people, be messengers of ruin to thee?' In horror I rose at the thought; but then also, in horror at the thought, rose one that was sculptured on the bas-relief — a dying trumpeter. Solemnly from the field of battle he rose to his feet; and, unslinging his stony trumpet, carried it, in his dying anguish, to his stony lips — sounding once, and yet once again; proclamation that, in *thy* ears, oh baby! must have spoken from the battlements of death. Immediately deep shadows fell between us, and aboriginal silence. The choir had ceased to sing. The hoofs of our horses, the rattling of our harness, alarmed the graves no more. By horror the bas-relief had been unlocked into life. By horror we, that were so full of life, we men and our horses, with their fiery fore-legs rising in mid air to their everlasting gallop, were frozen to a bas-relief. Then a third time the trumpet sounded; the seals were taken off all pulses; life, and the frenzy of life, tore into their channels again; again the choir burst forth in sunny grandeur, as from the muffling of storms and darkness; again the thunderings of our horses carried temptation into the graves. One cry burst from our lips as the clouds, drawing off from the aisle, showed it empty before us — 'Whither has the infant fled? — is the young child caught up to God?' Lo! afar off, in a vast recess, rose three mighty windows to the clouds: and on a level with their summits, at height insuperable to man, rose an altar of purest alabaster. On its eastern face was trembling a crimson glory. Whence came *that*? Was it from the reddening dawn that now streamed *through* the windows? Was it from the crimson robes of the martyrs that were painted *on* the windows? Was it from the bloody bas-reliefs of earth? Whencesoever it were — there, within that crimson radiance, suddenly appeared a female head, and then a female figure. It was the child — now grown up to woman's height. Clinging to the horns of the altar, there she stood — sinking, rising, trembling, fainting, — raving, despairing; and behind the volume of incense that, night and day, streamed upwards from the altar, was seen the fiery font, and dimly was descried the outline of the dreadful being that should baptize her with the baptism of death. But by her side was kneeling her better angel, that hid his face with wings; that wept and pleaded for *her*; that prayed when *she* could *not*; that fought with heaven by tears for *her* deliverance; which also, as he raised his immortal countenance from his wings, I saw, by the glory in his eye, that he had won at last.

5.

Then rose the agitation, spreading through the infinite cathedral, to its agony; then was completed the passion of the mighty fugue. The golden tubes of the organ, which as yet had but sobbed and muttered at intervals — gleaming amongst clouds and surges of incense — threw up, as from fountains unfathomable, columns of heart-shattering music. Choir and anti-choir were filling fast with unknown voices. Thou also, Dying Trumpeter! — with thy love that was victorious, and thy anguish that was finishing, didst enter the tumult: trumpet and echo — farewell love, and farewell anguish — rang through the dreadful *sanctus*. We, that spread flight before us, heard the tumult, as of flight, mustering behind us. In fear we looked round for the unknown steps that, in flight or in pursuit, were gathering upon our own. Who were these that followed? The faces, which no man could count — whence were *they*? 'Oh, darkness of the grave!' I exclaimed, 'that from the crimson altar and from the fiery font wert visited with secret light — that wert searched by the effulgence in the angel's eye — were these indeed thy children? Pomps of life, that, from the burials of centuries, rose again to the voice of perfect joy, could it be *ye* that had wrapped me in the reflux of panic?' What ailed me, that I should fear when the triumphs of earth were advancing? Ah! Pariah heart within me, that couldst never hear the sound of joy without sullen whispers of treachery in ambush; that, from six years old, didst never hear the promise of perfect love, without seeing aloft amongst the stars fingers as of a man's hand, writing the secret legend — '*Ashes to ashes, dust to dust!*' — wherefore shouldst *thou* not fear, though all men should rejoice? Lo! as I looked back for seventy leagues through the mighty cathedral, and saw the quick and the dead that sang together to God, together that sang to the generations of man — ah! raving, as of torrents that opened on every side: trepidation, as of female and infant steps that fled — ah! rushing, as of wings that chase! But I heard a voice from heaven, which said — 'Let there be no reflux of panic — let there be no more fear, and no more sudden death! Cover them with joy as the tides cover the shore!' *That* heard the children of the choir, *that* heard the children of the grave. All the hosts of jubilation made ready to move. Like armies that ride in pursuit, they moved with one step. Us, that, with laurelled heads, were passing from the cathedral through its eastern gates, they overtook, and, as with a garment, they wrapped us round with thunders that overpowered our own. As brothers we moved together; to the skies we rose — to the dawn that advanced — to the stars that fled; rendering thanks to God in the highest — that, having hid his face through one generation behind thick clouds of War, once again was ascending — was ascending from Waterloo — in the visions of Peace: rendering thanks for thee, young girl! whom having overshadowed with his ineffable passion of death — suddenly did God relent;

suffered thy angel to turn aside his arm ; and even in thee, sister unknown ! shown to me for a moment only to be hidden for ever, found an occasion to glorify his goodness. A thousand times, amongst the phantoms of sleep, has he shown thee to me, standing before the golden dawn, and ready to enter its gates — with the dreadful word going before thee — with the armies of the grave behind thee ; shown thee to me, sinking, rising, fluttering, fainting, but then suddenly reconciled, adoring : a thousand times has he followed thee in the worlds of sleep — through storms ; through desert seas ; through the darkness of quicksands ; through fugues and the persecution of fugues ; through dreams, and the dreadful resurrections that are in dreams — only that at the last, with one motion of his victorious arm, he might record and emblazon the endless resurrections of his love !

DINNER, REAL AND REPUTED.

GREAT misconceptions have always prevailed about the Roman *dinner*. Dinner [*cœna*] was the only meal which the Romans as a nation took. It was no accident, but arose out of their whole social economy. This we shall show by running through the history of a Roman day. *Ridentem dicere verum quid vetat?* And the course of this review will expose one or two important truths in ancient political economy, which have been wholly overlooked.

With the lark it was that the Roman rose. Not that the earliest lark rises so early in Latium as the earliest lark in England; that is, during summer: but then, on the other hand, neither does it ever rise so late. The Roman citizen was stirring with the dawn — which, allowing for the shorter longest-day and longer shortest-day of Rome, you may call about four in summer — about seven in winter. Why did he do this? Because he went to bed at a very early hour. But why did he do that? By backing in this way, we shall surely back into the very well of truth: always, if it is possible, let us have the *pourquoi* of the *pourquoi*. The Roman went to bed early for two special reasons. 1st, Because in Rome, which had been built for a martial destiny, every habit of life had reference to the usages of war. Every citizen, if he were not a mere proletarian animal kept at the public cost, held himself a sort of soldier-elect: the more noble he was, the more was his liability to military service: in short, all Rome, and at all times, was consciously 'in procinct.'[1] Now it was a principle of ancient warfare, that every hour of daylight had a triple worth, if valued against hours of darkness. That was one reason — a reason suggested by the understanding. But there was a second reason, far more remarkable; and this was a reason dictated by a blind necessity. It is an important fact, that this planet on which we live, this little industrious earth of ours, has developed her wealth by slow stages of increase. She was far from being the rich little globe in Cæsar's days that she is at present. The earth in our days is incalculably richer, as a whole, than in the time of Charlemagne: at that time she was richer, by many a million of acres, than in the era of Augustus. In that Augustan era we descry a clear belt of cultivation, averaging about six hundred miles in depth, running in a ring-fence about the Mediterranean. This belt, *and no more*, was in decent cultivation. Beyond that belt, there was only a wild Indian cultivation. At present what a difference! We have that very belt, but much richer, all things considered *æquatis æquandis*, than in the Roman era. The reader must not look to single cases, as that of Egypt or other parts of Africa, but take the whole collectively. On that scheme of valuation, we have the old Roman belt, the Mediterranean riband not much tarnished, and we have all the rest of

Europe to boot — or, speaking in scholar's language, as a *lucro ponamus*. We say nothing of remoter gains. Such being the case, our mother, the earth, being (as a whole) so incomparably poorer, could not in the Pagan era support the expense of maintaining great empires in cold latitudes. Her purse would not reach that cost. Wherever she undertook in those early ages to rear man in great abundance, it must be where nature would consent to work in partnership with herself; where *warmth* was to be had for nothing; where *clothes* were not so entirely indispensable but that a ragged fellow might still keep himself warm; where slight *shelter* might serve; and where the *soil*, if not absolutely richer in reversionary wealth, was more easily cultured. Nature must come forward liberally, and take a number of shares in every new joint-stock concern before it could move. Man, therefore, went to bed early in those ages, simply because his worthy mother earth could not afford him candles. She, good old lady, (or good young lady, for geologists know not[2] whether she is in that stage of her progress which corresponds to gray hairs, or to infancy, or to 'a *certain* age,') — she, good lady, would certainly have shuddered to hear any of her nations asking for candles. 'Candles!' She would have said, 'Who ever heard of such a thing? and with so much excellent daylight running to waste, as I have provided *gratis!* What will the wretches want next?'

The daylight, furnished *gratis*, was certainly 'neat,' and 'undeniable' in its quality, and quite sufficient for all purposes that were honest. Seneca, even in his own luxurious period, called those men '*lucifugæ*,' and by other ugly names, who lived chiefly by candle-light. None but rich and luxurious men, nay even amongst these, none but idlers *did* live much by candle-light. An immense majority of men in Rome never lighted a candle, unless sometimes in the early dawn. And this custom of Rome was the custom also of all nations that lived round the great pond of the Mediterranean. In Athens, Egypt, Palestine, Asia Minor, everywhere, the ancients went to bed, like good boys, from seven to nine o'clock.[3] The Turks and other people, who have succeeded to the stations and the habits of the ancients, do so at this day.

The Roman, therefore, who saw no joke in sitting round a table in the dark, went off to bed as the darkness began. Everybody did so. Old Numa Pompilius himself, was obliged to trundle off in the dusk. Tarquinius might be a very superb fellow ; but we doubt whether he ever saw a farthing rushlight. And, though it may be thought that plots and conspiracies would flourish in such a city of darkness, it is to be considered, that the conspirators themselves had no more candles than honest men : both parties were in the dark.

Being up then, and stirring not long after the lark, what mischief did the Roman go about first? Now-a-days, he would have taken a pipe or a cigar. But, alas for the ignorance of the poor heathen creatures! they had neither one nor the other. In this point, we must tax our mother earth with being really *too* stingy. In the case of the candles, we approve of her parsimony. Much mischief is brewed by candle-light. But, it was coming it too strong to allow no tobacco. Many a wild fellow in Rome, your Gracchi, Syllas, Catilines, would not have played 'h— and Tommy' in the way they did, if they could have soothed their angry stomachs with a cigar — a pipe has intercepted many an evil scheme. But the thing is passed helping now. At Rome, you must do as 'they does' at Rome. So, after shaving, (supposing the age of the *Barbati* to be passed,) what is the first business that our Roman will undertake? Forty to one he is a poor man, born to look upwards to his fellow-men — and not to look down upon anybody but slaves. He goes, therefore, to the palace of some grandee, some top-sawyer of the Senatorian order. This great man, for all his greatness, has turned out even sooner than himself. For he also has had no candles and no cigars; and he well knows, that before the sun looks into his portals, all his halls will be overflowing and buzzing with the matin susurrus of courtiers — the 'mane salutantes.'[4] It is as much as his popularity is worth to absent himself, or to keep people waiting. But surely, the reader may think, this poor man he might keep waiting. No, he might not; for, though poor, being a citizen, he is a gentleman. That was the consequence of keeping slaves. Wherever there is a class of slaves, he that enjoys the *jus suffragii* (no matter how poor) is a gentleman. The true Latin word for a gentleman is *ingenuus* — a freeman and the son of a freeman.

Yet even here there *were* distinctions. Under the Emperors, the courtiers were divided into two classes: with respect to the superior class, it was said of the sovereign — that he *saw* them, (*videbat;*) with respect to the other — that he *was seen*, ('*videbatur.*') Even Plutarch mentions it as a common boast in his times, ἡμας ειδεν ὁ βασιλευς — *Cæsar is in the habit of seeing me;* or, as a common plea for evading a suit, ἑτερους ὁρᾳ μαλλον — *I am sorry to say he is more inclined to look upon others.* And this usage derived itself (mark that well!) from the *republican* era. The aulic spirit was propagated by the Empire, but from a republican root.

Having paid his court, you will suppose that our friend comes home to breakfast. Not at all: no such discovery as 'breakfast' had then been made: breakfast was not invented for many centuries after that. We have always admired, and always shall admire, as the very best of all human stories, Charles Lamb's account of the origin of *roast pig* in China. Ching Ping, it seems, had suffered his father's house to be burned down: the outhouses were burned along with the house: and in one of these the pigs, by accident, were roasted to a turn. Memorable were the results for all future China and future civilization. Ping, who (like all China beside) had hitherto eaten his pig raw, now for the first time tasted it in a state of torrefaction. Of course he made his peace with his father by a part (tradition says a leg) of the new dish. The father was so astounded with the discovery, that he burned his house down once a year for the sake of coming at an annual banquet of roast pig. A curious prying sort of fellow, one Chang Pang, got to know of this. He also burned down a house with a pig in it, and had his eyes opened. The secret was ill kept — the discovery spread — many great conversions were made — houses were blazing in every part of the Celestial Empire. The insurance offices took the matter up. One Chong Pong, detected in the very act of shutting up a pig in his drawing-room, and then firing a train, was indicted on a charge of arson. The chief justice of Pekin, on that occasion, requested an officer of the court to hand him a piece of the roast pig, the *corpus delicti*, for pure curiosity led him to taste; but within two days after it was observed that his lordship's town-house was burned down. In short, all China apostatized to the new faith; and it was not until some centuries had passed, that a great genius arose, who established the second era in the history of roast pig, by showing that it could be had without burning down a house.

No such genius had yet arisen in Rome. Breakfast was not suspected. No prophecy, no type of breakfast had been published. In fact, it took as much time and research to arrive at that great discovery as at the Copernican system. True it is, reader, that you have heard of such a word as *jentaculum;* and your dictionary translates that old heathen word by the Christian word *breakfast.* But dictionaries, one and all, are dull deceivers. Between *jentaculum* and *breakfast* the differences are as wide as between a horse-chestnut and chestnut horse; differences in the *time when*, in the *place where*, in the *manner how*, but preëminently in the *thing which.*

Galen is a good authority upon such a subject, since, if (like other pagans) he ate no breakfast himself, in some sense he may be called the cause of breakfast to other men, by treating of those things which could safely be taken upon an empty stomach. As to the time, he (like many other authors) says, *περι τριτην, η (το μακροτερον) περι τεταρτην*, about the third, or at farthest about the fourth hour: and so exact is he, that he assumes the day to lie exactly between six and six o'clock, and to be divided into thirteen equal portions. So the time will be a few minutes before nine, or a few minutes before ten, in the forenoon. That seems fair enough. But it is not time in respect to its location that we are so much concerned with, as time in respect to its duration. Now, heaps of authorities take it for granted, that you are not to sit down — you are to stand; and, as to the place, that any place will do — 'any corner of the forum,' says Galen, 'any corner that you fancy:' which is like referring a man for his *salle à manger* to Westminster Hall or Fleet Street. Augustus, in a letter still surviving, tells us that he *jentabat*, or took his *jentaculum* in his carriage; now in a wheel carriage, (*in essedo*,) now in a litter or palanquin (*in lecticâ*.) This careless and disorderly way as to time and place, and other circumstances of haste, sufficiently indicate the quality of the meal you are to expect. Already you are 'sagacious of your quarry from so far.' Not that we would presume, excellent reader, to liken you to Death, or to insinuate that you are 'a grim feature.' But would it not make a saint 'grim,' to hear of such preparations for the morning meal? And then to hear of such consummations as *panis siccus*, dry bread; or, (if the learned reader thinks it will taste better in Greek,) *αρτος ξηρος!* And what may this word *dry* happen to mean? 'Does it mean stale bread?' says Salmasius. 'Shall we suppose,' says he, in querulous words, '*molli et recenti opponi*,' and from that antithesis conclude it to be, '*durum et non recens coctum, eoque sicciorem?*' Hard and stale, and for that reason the more arid!

Not quite so bad as that, we hope. Or again — '*siccum pro biscocto, ut hodie vocamus, sumemus?*'[5] By *hodie* Salmasius means, amongst his countrymen of France, where *biscoctus* is verbatim reproduced in the word *bis* (twice) *cuit*, (baked;) whence our own *biscuit*. Biscuit might do very well, could we be sure that it was cabin biscuit: but Salmasius argues — that in this case he takes it to mean '*buccellatum, qui est panis nauticus;*' that is, the ship company's biscuit, broken with a sledge-hammer. In Greek for the benefit again of the learned reader, it is termed διπυρος, indicating that it has passed twice under the action of fire.

'Well,' you say, 'no matter if it had passed fifty times — and through the fires of Moloch; only let us have this biscuit, such as it is.' In good faith, then, fasting reader, you are not likely to see much more than you *have* seen. It is a very Barmecide feast, we do assure you — this same 'jentaculum;' at which abstinence and patience are much more exercised than the teeth: faith and hope are the chief graces cultivated, together with that species of the *magnificum* which is founded on the *ignotum*. Even this biscuit was allowed in the most limited quantities; for which reason it is that the Greeks called this apology for a meal by the name of βουκκισμος, a word formed (as many words were in the Post-Augustan ages) from a Latin word — viz., *buccea*, a mouthful; not literally such, but so much as a polished man could allow himself to put into his mouth at once. 'We took a mouthful,' says Sir William Waller, the Parliamentary general, 'took a mouthful; paid our reckoning; mounted; and were off.' But there Sir William means, by his plausible 'mouthful,' something very much beyond either nine or nineteen ordinary quantities of that denomination, whereas the Roman 'jentaculum' was literally such; and, accordingly, one of the varieties under which the ancient vocabularies express this model of evanescent quantities is *gustatio*, a mere tasting; and again it is called by another variety, *gustus*, a mere taste: [whence by the usual suppression of the *s*, comes the French word for a collation or luncheon, viz. *gouter*.] Speaking of his uncle, Pliny the Younger says — 'Post solem plerumque lavabatur: deinde gustabat; dormiebat minimum; mox, quasi alio die, studebat in cœnæ tempus.' 'After taking the air he bathed; after that he broke his fast on a bit of biscuit, and took a very slight *siesta:* which done, as if awaking to a new day, he set in regularly to his studies, and pursued them to dinner-time.' *Gustabat* here meant that nondescript meal which arose at Rome when *jentaculum* and *prandium* were fused into one, and that only a *taste* or mouthful of biscuit, as we shall show farther on.

Possibly, however, most excellent reader, like some epicurean traveller, who, in crossing the Alps, finds himself weather-bound at St. Bernard's on Ash-Wednesdsy, you surmise a remedy: you descry some opening from 'the loopholes of retreat,' through which a few delicacies might be insinuated to spread verdure on this arid desert of biscuit. Casuistry can do much. A dead hand at casuistry has often proved more than a match for Lent with all his quarantines. But sorry we are to say that, in this case, no relief is hinted at in any ancient author. A grape or two, (not a bunch of grapes,) a raisin or two, a date, an olive — these are the whole amount of relief[6] which the chancery of the Roman kitchen granted in such cases. All things here hang together, and prove each other; the time, the place, the mode, the thing. Well might man eat standing, or eat in public, such a trifle as this. Go home to such a breakfast as this! You would as soon think of ordering a cloth to be laid in order to eat a peach, or of asking a friend to join you in an orange. No man makes 'two bites of a cherry.' So let us pass on to the other stages of the day. Only in taking leave of this morning stage, throw your eyes back with us, Christian reader, upon this truly heathen meal, fit for idolatrous dogs like your Greeks and your Romans; survey, through the vista of ages, that thrice-cursed biscuit, with half a fig, perhaps, by way of garnish, and a huge hammer by its side, to secure the certainty of mastication, by previous comminution. Then turn your eyes to a Christian breakfast — hot rolls, eggs, coffee, beef; but down, down, rebellious visions: we need say no more! You, reader, like ourselves, will breathe a malediction on the classical era, and thank your stars for making you a Romanticist. Every morning we thank ours for keeping us back, and reserving us to an age in which breakfast had been already invented. In the words of Ovid we say: —

> 'Prisca juvent alios: ego me nunc denique natum
> Gratulor. Hæc ætas moribus apta meis.'

Our friend, the Roman cit, has therefore thus far, in his progress through life, obtained no breakfast, if he ever contemplated an idea so frantic. But it occurs to you, our faithful reader, that perhaps he will not always be thus unhappy. We could bring waggon-loads of sentiments, Greek as well as Roman, which prove, more clearly than the most eminent pikestaff, that, as the wheel of fortune revolves, simply out of the fact that it has carried a man downwards, it must subsequently carry him upwards, no matter what dislike that wheel, or any of its spokes, may bear to that man: 'non, si male nunc sit, et olim sic erit:' and that if a man, through the madness of his nation, misses coffee and hot rolls at nine, he may easily run into a leg of mutton at twelve. True it is he may do so: truth is commendable: and we will not deny that a man may sometimes, by losing a breakfast, gain a dinner. Such things have been in various ages, and will be again, but not at Rome. There are reasons against it. We have heard of men who consider life under the idea of a wilderness — dry as 'a remainder biscuit after a voyage:' and who consider a day under the idea of a little life. Life is the *ma*crocosm, or world at large: day is the *mi*crocosm, or world in miniature. Consequently, if life is a wilderness, then day, as a little life, is a little wilderness. And this wilderness can be safely traversed only by having relays of fountains, or stages for refreshment. Such stages, they conceive, are found in the several meals which Providence has stationed at due intervals through the day, whenever the perverseness of man does not break the chain, or derange the order of succession.

These are the anchors by which man rides in that billowy ocean between morning and night. The first anchor, viz., breakfast, having given way in Rome, the more need there is that he should pull up by the second; and that is often reputed to be dinner. And as your dictionary, good reader, translated *breakfast* by that vain word *jentaculum*, so, doubtless, it will translate *dinner* by that still vainer word *prandium*. Sincerely we hope that your own dinner on this day, and through all time coming, may have a better root in fact and substance than this most visionary of all baseless things — the Roman *prandium*, of which we shall presently show you that the most approved translation is *moonshine*.

Reader, we are not jesting here. In the very spirit of serious truth, we assure you, that the delusion about 'jentaculum' is even exceeded by this other delusion about 'prandium.' Salmasius himself, for whom a natural prejudice of place and time partially obscured the truth, admits, however, that *prandium* was a meal which the ancients rarely took; his very words are — '*raro prandebant veteres.*' Now, judge for yourself of the good sense which is shown in translating by the word *dinner*, which must of necessity mean the chief meal — a Roman word which represents a fancy meal, a meal of caprice, a meal which few people took. At this moment, what is the single point of agreement between the noon meal of the English laborer and the evening meal of the English gentleman? What is the single circumstance common to both, which causes us to denominate them by the common name of *dinner*? It is that in both we recognize the *principal* meal of the day, the meal upon which is thrown the *onus* of the day's support. In everything else they are as wide asunder as the poles; but they agree in this one point of their function. It is credible that, to represent such a meal amongst ourselves, we select a Roman word so notoriously expressing a mere shadow, a pure apology, that very few people ever tasted it — nobody sate down to it — not many washed their hands after it, and gradually the very name of it became interchangeable with another name, implying the slightest possible act of trying or sipping? '*Post lavationem sine mensâ prandium*,' says Seneca, '*post quod non sunt lavandæ manus;*' that is, 'after bathing, I take a *prandium* without sitting down to table, and such a *prandium* as brings after itself no need of washing the hands.' No; moonshine as little soils the hands as it oppresses the stomach.

Reader! we, as well as Pliny, had an uncle, an East Indian uncle; doubtless you have such an uncle; everybody has an Indian uncle. Generally such a person is 'rather yellow, rather yellow,' [to quote Canning *versus* Lord Durham :] that is the chief fault with his physics; but, as to his morals, he is universally a man of princely aspirations and habits. He is not always so orientally rich as he is reputed; but he is always orientally munificent. Call upon him at any hour from two to five, he insists on your taking *tiffin:* and such a tiffin! The English corresponding term is luncheon: but how meagre a shadow is the European meal to its glowing Asiatic cousin! Still, gloriously as tiffin shines, does anybody imagine that it is a vicarious dinner, or ever meant to be the substitute of dinner? Wait till eight, and you will have your eyes opened on that subject. So of the Roman *prandium:*

had it been as luxurious as it was simple, still it was always viewed as something meant only to stay the stomach, as a prologue to something beyond. The *prandium* was far enough from giving the feeblest idea of the English luncheon; yet it stood in the same relation to the Roman day. Now to English*men* that meal scarcely exists; and were it not for women, whose delicacy of organization does not allow them to fast so long as men, would probably be abolished. It is singular in this, as in other points, how nearly England and ancient Rome approximate. We all know how hard it is to tempt a man generally into spoiling his appetite, by eating before dinner. The same dislike of violating what they called the integrity of the appetite, [*integram famem*,] existed at Rome. Every man who knows anything of Latin critically, sees the connection of the word *integer* with *in* and *tetigi*: *integer* means what is *intact*, unviolated by touch. Cicero, when protesting against spoiling his appetite for dinner, by tasting anything beforehand, says, *integram famem ad cœnam afferam*; I shall bring to dinner an appetite untampered with. Nay, so much stress did the Romans lay on maintaining this primitive state of the appetite undisturbed, that any prelusions with either *jentaculum* or *prandium* were said, by a very strong phrase indeed, *polluere famem*, to pollute the sanctity of the appetite. The appetite was regarded as a holy vestal flame, soaring upwards towards dinner throughout the day: if undebauched, it tended to its natural consummation in *cœna*: expired like a phœnix, to rise again out of its own ashes. On this theory, to which language had accommodated itself, the two prelusive meals of nine o'clock, A. M., and of one, P. M., so far from being ratified by the public sense, and adopted into the economy of the day, were regarded gloomily as gross irregularities, enormities, debauchers of the natural instinct; and, in so far as they thwarted that instinct, lessened it, or depraved it, were universally held to be full of pollution; and, finally, to *profane* a motion of nature. Such was the language.

But we guess what is passing in the reader's mind. He thinks that all this proves the *prandium* to have been a meal of little account; and in very many cases absolutely unknown. But still he thinks all this might happen to the English dinner — *that* might be neglected; supper might be generally preferred; and, nevertheless, dinner would be as truly entitled to the name of dinner as before. Many a student neglects his dinner; enthusiasm in any pursuit must often have extinguished appetite for all of us. Many a time and oft did this happen to Sir Isaac Newton. Evidence is on record, that such a deponent at eight o'clock, A. M., found Sir Isaac with one stocking on, one off; at two, said deponent called him to dinner. Being interrogated whether Sir Isaac had pulled on the *minus* stocking, or gartered the *plus* stocking, witness replied that he had not. Being asked if Sir Isaac came to dinner, replied that he did not. Being again asked, 'At sunset, did you look in on Sir Isaac?' Witness replied, 'I did.' 'And now, upon your conscience, sir, by the virtue of your oath, in what state were the stockings?' *Ans.* '*In statu quo ante bellum.*' It seems Sir Isaac had fought through that whole battle of a long day, so trying a campaign to many people — he had traversed that whole sandy Zaarah, without calling, or needing to call at one of those fountains, stages, or *mansiones*,[7] by which (according to our former explanation) Providence has relieved the continuity of arid soil, which else disfigures that long dreary level. This happens to all; but was dinner not dinner, and did supper become dinner, because Sir Isaac Newton ate nothing at the first, and threw the whole day's support upon the last? No, you will say, a rule is not defeated by one casual deviation, nor by one person's constant deviation. Everybody else was still dining at two, though Sir Isaac might not; and Sir Isaac himself on most days no more deferred his dinner beyond two, than he sate with one stocking off. But what if everybody, Sir Isaac included, had deferred his substantial meal until night, and taken a slight refection only at two? The question put does really represent the very case which has happened with us in England. In 1700, a large part of London took a meal at two, P. M., and another at seven or eight, P. M. In 1839, a large part of London is still doing the very same thing, taking one meal at two, and another at seven or eight. But the names are entirely changed: the two o'clock meal used to be called *dinner*, and is now called *luncheon;* the eight o'clock meal used to be called *supper*, and is now called *dinner*.

Now the question is easily solved: because, upon reviewing the idea of dinner, we soon perceive that time has little or no connection with it: since, both in England and France, dinner has travelled, like the hand of a clock, through *every* hour between ten, A. M.

and ten, P. M. We have a list, well attested, of every successive hour between these limits having been the known established hour for the royal dinner-table within the last three hundred and fifty years. Time, therefore, vanishes from the equation: it is a quantity as regularly exterminated as in any algebraic problem. The true elements of the idea, are evidently these: — 1. That dinner is that meal, no matter when taken, which is the principal meal; *i. e.* the meal on which the day's support is thrown. 2. That it is the meal of hospitality. 3. That it is the meal (with reference to both Nos. 1 and 2) in which animal food predominates. 4. That it is that meal which, upon necessity arising for the abolition of all *but* one, would naturally offer itself as that one. Apply these four tests to *prandium*: — How could that meal answer to the first test, as *the day's support*, which few people touched? How could that meal answer to the second test, as the *meal of hospitality*, at which nobody sate down? How could that meal answer to the third test, as the meal of animal food, which consisted exclusively and notoriously of bread? Or to the fourth test, of the meal *entitled to survive the abolition of the rest*, which was itself abolished at all times in practice?

Tried, therefore, by every test, *prandium* vanishes. But we have something further to communicate about this same *prandium*.

I. It came to pass, by a very natural association of feeling, that *prandium* and *jentaculum*, in the latter centuries of Rome, were generally confounded. This result was inevitable. Both professed the same basis. Both came in the morning. Both were fictions. Hence they were confounded.

That fact speaks for itself, — breakfast and luncheon never could have been confounded ; but who would be at the pains of distinguishing two shadows ? In a gambling-house of that class, where you are at liberty to sit down to a splendid banquet, anxiety probably prevents your sitting down at all ; but, if you do, the same cause prevents your noticing what you eat. So of the two *pseudo* meals of Rome, they came in the very midst of the Roman business ; viz. from nine, A. M. to two, P. M. Nobody could give his mind to them, had they been of better quality. There lay one cause of their vagueness, viz. — in their position. Another cause was, the common basis of both. Bread was so notoriously the predominating 'feature' in each of these prelusive banquets, that all foreigners at Rome, who communicated with Romans through the Greek language, knew both the one and the other by the name of ἀρτοσιτος, or the *bread repast.* Originally this name had been restricted to the earlier meal. But a distinction without a difference could not sustain itself: and both alike disguised their emptiness under this pompous quadrisyllable. In the identity of substance, therefore, lay a second ground of confusion. And, then, thirdly, even as to the time, which had ever been the sole real distinction, there arose from accident a tendency to converge. For it happened that while some had *jentaculum* but no *prandium*, others had *prandium* but no *jentaculum ;* a third party had both ; a fourth party, by much the largest, had neither. Out of which varieties (who would think that a nonentity could cut up into so many somethings ?) arose a fifth party of compromisers, who, because they could not afford a regular *cœna*, and yet were hospitably disposed, fused the two ideas into one; and so, because the usual time for the idea of a breakfast was nine to ten, and for the idea of a luncheon twelve to one, compromised the rival pretensions by what diplomatists call a *mezzo termine;* bisecting the time at eleven, and melting the two ideas into one. But by thus merging the separate times of each, they abolished the sole real difference that had ever divided them. Losing that, they lost all.

Perhaps, as two negatives make one affirmative, it may be thought that two layers of moonshine might coalesce into one pancake; and two Barmecide banquets might compose one poached egg. Of that the company were the best judges. But probably, as a rump and dozen, in our land of wagers, is construed with a very liberal latitude as to the materials, so Martial's invitation, 'to take bread with him at eleven,' might be understood by the συνετοι as significant of something better than αρτοσιτος. Otherwise, in good truth, 'moonshine and turn-out' at eleven, A. M., would be even worse than 'tea and turn-out' at eight, P. M., which the 'fervida juventus' of young England so loudly detests. But however that might be, in this convergement of the several frontiers, and the confusion that ensued, one cannot wonder that, whilst the two bladders collapsed into one idea, they actually expanded into four names, two Latin and two Greek, *gustus* and *gustatio*, γευσις, and γευσμα, which all alike express the merely tentative or exploratory act of a *prægustator* or professional 'taster' in a king's household: what, if applied to a fluid, we should denominate sipping.

At last, by so many steps all in one direction, things

had come to such a pass — the two prelusive meals of the Roman morning, each for itself separately vague from the beginning, had so communicated and interfused their several and joint vaguenesses, that at last no man knew or cared to know what any other man included in his idea of either; how much or how little. And you might as well have hunted in the woods of Ethiopia for Prester John, or fixed the parish of the everlasting Jew,[8] as have attempted to say what 'jentaculum' might be, or what 'prandium.' Only one thing was clear — what they were *not*. Neither was or wished to be anything that people cared for. They were both empty shadows; but shadows as they were, we find from Cicero that they had a power of polluting and profaning better things than themselves.

We presume that no rational man will henceforth look for 'dinner' — that great idea according to Dr. Johnson — that sacred idea according to Cicero — in a bag of moonshine on one side, or a bag of pollution on the other. *Prandium*, so far from being what our foolish dictionaries pretend — dinner itself — never in its palmiest days was more or other than a miserable attempt at being *luncheon*. It was a *conatus*, what physiologists call a *nisus*, a struggle in a very ambitious spark, or *scintilla*, to kindle into a fire. This *nisus* went on for some centuries; but finally issued in smoke. If *prandium* had worked out his ambition, had 'the great stream of tendency' accomplished all his wishes, *prandium* never could have been more than a very indifferent luncheon. But now,

II. We have to offer another fact, ruinous to our dictionaries on another ground. Various circumstances have disguised the truth, but a truth it is, that 'prandium,' in its very origin and *incunabula*, never was a meal known to the Roman *culina*. In that court it was never recognized except as an alien. It had no original domicile in the city of Rome. It was a *vox castrensis*, a word and an idea purely martial, and pointing to martial necessities. Amongst the new ideas proclaimed to the recruit, this was one — 'Look for no "*cœna*," no regular dinner, with us. Resign these unwarlike notions. It is true that even war has its respites; in these it would be possible to have our Roman *cœna* with all its equipage of ministrations. Such luxury untunes the mind for doing and suffering. Let us voluntarily renounce it; that when a necessity of renouncing it arrives, we may not feel it among the hardships of war. From the day when you enter the gates of the camp, reconcile yourself, tyro, to a new fashion of meal, to what in camp dialect we call *prandium*.' This 'prandium,' this essentially military meal, was taken standing, by way of symbolizing the necessity of being always ready for the enemy. Hence the posture in which it was taken at Rome, the very counter-pole to the luxurious posture of dinner. A writer of the third century, a period from which the Romans naturally looked back upon everything connected with their own early habits, and with the same kind of interest as we extend to our Alfred, (separated from us as Romulus from them by just a thousand years,) in speaking of *prandium*, says, 'Quod dictum est *parandium*, ab eo quod milites ad bellum *paret*.' Isidorus again says, 'Proprie apud veteres prandium vocatum fuisse omnem militum cibum ante pugnam;' *i. e.* 'that, properly speaking, amongst our ancestors every military meal taken before battle was termed *prandium*.' According to Isidore, the proposition is reciprocating, viz., that, as every *prandium* was a military meal, so every military meal was called *prandium*. But, in fact, the reason of that is apparent. Whether in the camp or the city, the early Romans had probably but one meal in a day. That is true of many a man amongst ourselves by choice; it is true also, to our knowledge, of some horse regiments in our service, and may be of all. This meal was called *cœna*, or dinner in the city — *prandium* in camps. In the city it would always be tending to one fixed hour. In the camp innumerable accidents of war would make it very uncertain. On this account it would be an established rule to celebrate the daily meal at noon, if nothing hindered; not that a later hour would not have been preferred had the choice been free; but it was better to have a certainty at a bad hour, than by waiting for a better hour to make it an uncertainty. For it was a camp proverb — *Pransus, paratus;* armed with his daily meal, the soldier is ready for service. It was not, however, that all meals, as Isidore imagined, were indiscriminately called *prandium;* but that the one sole meal of the day, by accidents of war, might, and did, revolve through all hours of the day.

The first introduction of this military meal into Rome itself, would be through the honorable pedantry of old centurions, &c., delighting (like the *Trunnions*, &c., of our navy) to keep up in peaceful life some image or memorial of their past experience, so wild, so full of peril, excitement, and romance, as Roman warfare must have been in those ages. Many non-military people for health's sake, many as an excuse for eating early, many by way of interposing some refreshment between the stages of forensic business, would adopt this hurried and informal meal. Many would wish to see their sons adopting such a meal as a training for foreign service in particular, and for temperance in general. It would also be maintained by a solemn and very interesting commemoration of this camp repast in Rome.

This commemoration, because it has been grossly misunderstood by Salmasius, (whose error arose from not marking the true point of a particular antithesis,) and still more, because it is a distinct confirmation of all we have said as to the military nature of *prandium*, we shall detach from the series of our illustrations, by placing it in a separate paragraph.

On a set day the officers of the army were invited by Cæsar to a banquet; it was a circumstance expressly noticed in the invitation, by the proper officers of the palace, that the banquet was not a 'cœna,' but a 'prandium.' What followed, in consequence? Why, that all the guests sate down in full military accoutrement; whereas, observes the historian, had it been a *cœna*, the officers would have unbelted their swords; for he adds, even in Cæsar's presence the officers lay aside their swords. The word *prandium*, in short, converted the palace into the imperial tent; and Cæsar was no longer a civil emperor and *princeps senătûs*, but became a commander-in-chief amongst a council of his staff, all belted and plumed, and in full military fig.

On this principle we come to understand why it is, that, whenever the Latin poets speak of an army as taking food, the word used is always *prandens*, and *pransus ;* and, when the word used is *prandens*, then always it is an army that is concerned. Thus Juvenal in a well-known satire —

——— 'Credimus altos
Desiccasse amnes, epotaque flumina, Medo *Prandente*.'

Not *cœnante*, observe : you might as well talk of an army taking tea and toast. Nor is that word ever applied to armies. It is true that the converse is not so rigorously observed ; nor ought it, from the explanations already given. Though no soldier dined, (*cœnabat*,) yet the citizen sometimes adopted the camp usage and took a *prandium*. But generally the poets use the word merely to mark the time of day. In that most humorous appeal of Perseus — 'Cur quis non prandeat, hoc est ? ' 'Is this a sufficient reason for losing one's *prandium* ? ' He was obliged to say *prandium*, because no exhibitions ever could cause a man to lose his *cœna*, since none were displayed at a time of day when anybody in Rome would have attended. Just as, in alluding to a parliamentary speech notoriously delivered at midnight, an English satirist must have said, Is this a speech to furnish an argument for leaving one's bed ? — not as what stood foremost in his regard, but as the only thing that *could* be lost at the time of night.

On this principle, also, viz. by going back to the military origin of *prandium*, we gain the interpretation of all the peculiarities attached to it ; viz. — 1, its early hour — 2, its being taken in a standing posture —

3, in the open air — 4, the humble quality of its materials — bread and biscuit, (the main articles of military fare.) In all these circumstances of the meal, we read, most legibly written, the exotic and military character of the meal.

Thus we have brought down our Roman friend to noonday, or even one hour later than noon, and to this moment the poor man has had nothing to eat. For, supposing him to be not *impransus*, and supposing him *jentâsse* beside ; yet it is evident, (we hope,) that neither one nor the other means more than what it was often called, viz. βυκκισμος, or, in plain English, a mouthful. How long do we intend to keep him waiting ? Reader, he will dine at three, or (supposing dinner put off to the latest) at four. Dinner was never known to be later than the tenth hour at Rome, which in summer would be past five ; but for a far greater proportion of days would be near four in Rome, except for one or two of the emperors, whom the mere business attached to their unhappy station kept sometimes dinnerless till six. And so entirely was a Roman the creature of ceremony, that a national mourning would probably have been celebrated, and the 'sad augurs' would have been called in to expiate the prodigy, had the general dinner lingered beyond four.

But, meantime, what has our friend been about since perhaps six or seven in the morning ? After paying his little homage to his *patronus*, in what way has he fought with the great enemy Time since then ? Why, reader, this illustrates one of the most interesting features in the Roman character. The Roman was the idlest of men. 'Man and boy,' he was 'an idler in the land.' He called himself and his pals 'rerum dominos, gentemque togatam;' *the gentry that wore the toga.*' Yes, and a pretty affair that 'toga' was. Just figure to yourself, reader, the picture of a hard-working man, with horny hands, like our hedgers, ditchers, weavers, porters, &c., setting to work on the highroad in that vast sweeping toga, filling with a strong gale like the mainsail of a frigate. Conceive the roars with which this magnificent figure would be received into the bosom of a poor-house detachment sent out to attack the stones on some new line of road, or a fatigue party of dustmen sent upon secret service. Had there been nothing left as a memorial of the Romans but that one relic — their immeasurable toga,[9] we should have known that they were born and bred to idleness. In fact, except in war, the Roman never did anything at all but sun himself. *Ut se apricaret* was the final cause of peace in his opinion; in literal truth, that he might make an *apricot* of himself. The public rations at all times supported the poorest inhabitant of Rome if he were a citizen. Hence it was that Hadrian was so astonished with the spectacle of Alexandria, '*civitas opulenta, fæcunda, in quâ nemo vivat otiosus.*' Here first he saw the spectacle of a vast city, second only to Rome, where every man had something to do; '*podagrosi quod agant habent; habent cæci quod faciant; ne chiragrici*' (those with gout in the fingers) '*apud eos otiosi vivunt.*' No poor rates levied upon the rest of the world for the benefit of their own paupers were there distributed *gratis.* The prodigious spectacle (so it seemed to Hadrian) was exhibited in Alexandria, of all men earning their bread in the sweat of their brow. In Rome only, (and at one time in some of the Grecian states,) it was the very meaning of *citizen* that he should vote and be idle.

In these circumstances, where the whole sum of life's duties amounted to voting, all the business a man *could* have was to attend the public assemblies, electioneering, or factious. These, and any judicial trial (public or private) that might happen to interest him for the persons concerned, or for the questions, amused him through the morning; that is, from eight till one. He might also extract some diversion from the *columnæ*, or pillars of certain porticos to which they pasted advertisements. These *affiches* must have been numerous; for all the girls in Rome who lost a trinket or a pet bird, or a lap-dog, took this mode of angling in the great ocean of the public for the missing articles.

But all this time we take for granted that there were no shows in a course of exhibition, either the dreadful ones of the amphitheatre, or the bloodless ones of the circus. If there were, then that became the business of all Romans; and it was a business which would have occupied him from daylight until the light began to fail. Here we see another effect from the scarcity of artificial light amongst the ancients. These magnificent shows went on by daylight. But how incomparably better would have been the splendor by lamp-light! What a gigantic conception! Eighty thousand human faces all revealed under one blaze of lamp-light! Lord Bacon saw the mighty advantage of candle-light for the pomps and glories of this world.

But the poverty of the earth was the ultimate cause that the Pagan shows proceeded by day. Not that the masters of the world, who rained Arabian odors and perfumed waters of the most costly description from a thousand fountains, simply to cool the summer heats, would have regarded the expense of light; cedar and other odorous woods burning upon vast altars, together with every variety of fragrant torch, would have created light enough to shed a new day over the distant Adriatic.

However, as there are no public spectacles, we will suppose, and the courts of political meetings, (if not closed altogether by superstition,) would at any rate be closed in the ordinary course by twelve or one o'clock, nothing remains for him to do, before returning home, except perhaps to attend the *palæstra*, or some public recitation of a poem written by a friend, but in any case to attend the public baths. For these the time varied; and many people have thought it tyrannical in some of the Cæsars that they imposed restraints on the time open for the baths; some, for instance, would not suffer them to open at all before two, and in any case, if you were later than four or five in summer, you would have to pay a fine which most effectually cleaned out the baths of all raff, since it was a sum that *John Quires* could not have produced to save his life. But it should be considered that the emperor was the steward of the public resources for maintaining the baths in fuel, oil, attendance, repairs. We are prepared to show, on a fitting occasion, that every fourth person [10] amongst the citizens bathed daily, and non-citizens, of course, paid an *extra* sum. Now the population of Rome was far larger than has ever been hinted at except by Lipsius. But certain it is, that during the long peace of the first Cæsars, and after the *annonaria provisio*, (that great pledge of popularity to a Roman prince,) had been increased by the corn tribute from the Nile, the Roman population took an immense lurch ahead. The subsequent increase of baths, whilst no old ones were neglected, proves *that* decisively. And as citizenship expanded by means of the easy terms on which it could be had, so did the bathers multiply. The population of Rome in the century after Augustus, was far greater than during that era; and this, still acting as a vortex to the rest of the world, may have been one great motive with Constantine for 'transferring' the capital eastwards; in reality, for breaking up one monster capital into two or more manageable dimensions. Two o'clock was often the earliest hour at which the public baths were opened. But in Martial's time a man could go without blushing (*salvâ fronte*) at eleven, though even then two o'clock was the meridian hour for the great uproar of splashing, and swimming, and 'larking' in the endless baths of endless Rome.

And now, at last, bathing finished, and the exercises of the *palæstra*, at half-past two, or three, our friend finds his way home — not again to leave it for that day. He is now a new man; refreshed, oiled with perfumes, his dust washed off by hot water, and ready for enjoyment. These were the things that determined the time for dinner. Had there been no other proof that *cœna* was the Roman dinner, this is an ample one. Now first the Roman was fit for dinner, in a condition of luxurious ease; business over — that day's load of anxiety laid aside — his *cuticle*, as he delighted to talk, cleansed and polished — nothing more to do or to think of until the next morning, he might now go and dine, and get drunk with a safe conscience. Besides, if he does not get dinner now, when will he get it? For most demonstrably he has taken nothing yet which comes near in value to that basin of soup which many of ourselves take at the Roman hour of bathing. No; we have kept our man fasting as yet. It is to be hoped that something is coming at last.

It *does* come, — dinner, the great meal of '*cœna*;' the meal sacred to hospitality and genial pleasure, comes now to fill up the rest of the day, until light fails altogether.

Many people are of opinion that the Romans only understood what the capabilities of dinner were. It is certain that they were the first great people that discovered the true secret and meaning of dinner, the great office which it fulfils, and which we in England are now so generally acting on. Barbarous nations, — and none were, in that respect, more barbarous than our own ancestors, — made this capital blunder; the brutes, if you asked them what was the use of dinner, what it was meant for, stared at you and replied — as a horse would reply if you put the same question about his provender — that it was to give him strength for finishing his work! Therefore, if you point your telescope back to antiquity about twelve or one o'clock in the daytime, you will descry our most worthy ancestors all eating for their very lives, eating as dogs eat, viz. in bodily fear that some other dog will come and take their dinner away. What swelling of the veins in the temples! (see Boswell's natural history of Dr. Johnson at dinner;) what intense and rapid deglutition! what odious clatter of knives and plates! what silence of the human voice! what gravity! what fury in the libidinous eyes with which they contemplate the dishes! Positively it was an *indecent* spectacle to see Dr. Johnson at dinner. But, above all, what maniacal haste and hurry, as if the fiend were waiting with red-hot pincers to lay hold of the hindermost!

Oh, reader, do you recognize in this abominable picture your respected ancestors and ours? Excuse us for saying — 'What monsters!' We have a right to call our own ancestors monsters; and, if so, we must have the same right over yours. For Dr. Southey has shown plainly in the 'Doctor,' that every man having four grand-parents in the second stage of ascent, (each of whom having four, therefore,) sixteen in the third, and so on, long before you get to the Conquest, every man and woman then living in England will be wanted to make up the sum of my separate ancestors; consequently, you must take your ancestors out of the very same fund, or (if you are too proud for that) you must go without ancestors. So that, your ancestors being clearly mine, I have a right in law to call the whole 'kit' of them monsters. *Quod erat demonstrandum.* Really and upon our honor, it makes one, for the moment, ashamed of one's descent; one would wish to disinherit one's-self backwards, and (as Sheridan says in the *Rivals*) to 'cut the connection.' Wordsworth has an admirable picture in Peter Bell of 'A snug party in a parlor,' removed into *limbus patrum* for their offences in the flesh: —

'Cramming, as they on earth were cramm'd;
All sipping wine, all sipping tea;
But, as you by their faces see,
All *silent,* and all d — d.'

How well does that one word describe those venerable ancestral dinners — 'All silent!' Contrast this infernal silence of voice and fury of eye with the '*risus amabilis*,' the festivity, the social kindness, the music, the wine, the '*dulcis insania*,' of a Roman '*cœna*.' We mentioned four tests for determining what meal is, and what is not, dinner: we may now add a fifth, viz. the spirit of festal joy and elegant enjoyment, of anxiety laid aside, and of honorable social pleasure put on like a marriage garment.

And what caused the difference between our ancestors and the Romans? Simply this — the error of interposing dinner in the middle of business, thus courting all the breezes of angry feeling that may happen to blow from the business yet to come, instead of finishing, absolutely closing, the account with this world's troubles before you sit down. That unhappy interpolation ruined all. Dinner was an ugly little parenthesis between two still uglier clauses of a teetotally ugly sentence. Whereas with us, their enlightened posterity, to whom they have the honor to be ancestors, dinner is a great reaction. There lies our conception of the matter. It grew out of the very excess of the evil. When business was moderate, dinner was allowed to divide and bisect it. When it swelled into that vast strife and agony, as one may call it, that boils along the tortured streets of modern London or other capitals, men began to see the necessity of an adequate counterforce to push against this overwhelming torrent, and thus maintain the equilibrium. Were it not for the soft relief of a six o'clock dinner, the gentle manner succeeding to the boisterous hubbub of the day, the soft glowing lights, the wine, the intellectual conversation, life in London is now come to such a pass, that in two years all nerves would sink before it. But for this periodic reaction, the modern business which draws so cruelly on the brain, and so little on the hands, would overthrow that organ in all but those of coarse organization. Dinner it is, — meaning by dinner the whole complexity of attendant circumstances, — which saves the modern brain-working men from going mad.

This revolution as to dinner was the greatest in virtue and value ever accomplished. In fact, those are always the most operative revolutions which are brought about through social or domestic changes. A nation must be barbarous, neither could it have much intellectual business, which dined in the morning. They could not be at ease in the morning. So much *must* be granted: every day has its separate *quantum*, its dose (as the doctrinists of rent phrase it) of anxiety, that could not be digested so soon as noon. No man will say it. He, therefore, who dined at noon, was willing to sit down squalid as he was, with his dress unchanged, his cares not washed off. And what follows from that? Why, that to him, to such a canine or cynical specimen of the genus *homo*, dinner existed only as a physical event, a mere animal relief, a mere carnal enjoyment. For what, we demand, did this fleshly creature differ from the carrion crow, or the kite, or the vulture, or the cormorant? A French judge, in an action upon a wager, laid it down in law, that man only had a *bouche*, all other animals had a *gueule:* only with regard to the horse, in consideration of his beauty, nobility, use, and in honor of the respect with which man regarded him, by the courtesy of Christendom, he might be allowed to have a *bouche*, and his reproach of brutality, if not taken away, might thus be hidden. But surely, of the rabid animal who is caught dining at noonday, the *homo ferus*, who affronts the meridian sun like Thystes and Atreus, by his inhuman meals, we are, by parity of reason, entitled to say, that he has a 'maw,' (so has Milton's Death,) but nothing resembling stomach. And to this vile man a philosopher would say — 'Go away, sir, and come back to me two or three centuries hence, when you have learned to be a reasonable creature, and to make that physico-intellectual thing out of dinner which it was meant to be, and is capable of becoming.' In Henry VII.'s time the court dined at eleven in the forenoon. But even that hour was considered so shockingly late in the French court, that Louis XII. actually had his gray hairs brought down with sorrow to the grave, by changing his regular hour of half-past nine for eleven, in gallantry to his young English bride.[11] He fell a victim to late hours in the forenoon. In Cromwell's time they dined at one, P. M. One century and a half had carried them on by two hours. Doubtless, old cooks and scullions wondered what the world would come to next. Our French neighbors were in the same predicament. But they far surpassed us in veneration for the meal. They actually dated from it. Dinner constituted the great era of the day. *L'apres diner* is almost the sole date which you find in Cardinal De Retz's memoirs of the *Fronde.* Dinner was their *Hegira* — dinner was their *line* in traversing the ocean of day: they crossed the equator when they dined. Our English revolution came next; it made some little difference, we have heard people say, in Church and State; but its great effects were perceived in dinner. People now dined at two. So dined Addison for his last thirty years; so dined Pope, who was coeval with the revolution through his entire life. Precisely as the rebellion of 1745 arose, did people (but observe, very great people) advance to four, P. M. Philosophers, who watch the 'semina rerum,' and the first symptoms of change, had perceived this alternation singing in the upper air like a coming storm some little time before. About the year 1740, Pope complains to a friend of Lady Suffolk's dining so late as four. Young people may bear those things, he observes; but as to himself, now turned of fifty, if such doings went on, if Lady Suffolk would adopt such strange hours, he must really absent himself from Marble Hill. Lady Suffolk had a right to please herself; he himself loved her. But if she would persist, all which remained for a decayed poet was respectfully to 'cut his stick, and retire.' Whether Pope ever put up with four o'clock dinners again, we have vainly sought to fathom. Some things advance continuously, like a flood or a fire, which always make an end of A, eat and digest it, before they go on to B. Other things advance *per saltum* — they do not silently cancer their way onwards, but lie as still as a snake after they have made some notable conquest, then when unobserved they make themselves up 'for mischief,' and take a flying bound onwards. Thus advanced dinner, and by these fits got into the territory of evening. And ever as it made a motion onwards, it found the nation more civilized, (else the change would not have been effected,) and raised them to a still higher civilization. The next relay on that line of road, the next repeating frigate, is Cowper in his poem on *Conversation*. He speaks of four o'clock as still the elegant hour for dinner — the hour for the *lautiores* and the *lepidi homines*. Now this was written about 1780, or a little earlier; perhaps, therefore, just one generation after Pope's Lady Suffolk. But then Cowper was living amongst the rural gentry, not in high life; yet, again, Cowper was nearly connected by blood with the eminent Whig house of Cowper, and acknowledged as a kinsman. About twenty-five years after this, we may take Oxford as a good exponent of the national advance. As a magnificent body of 'foundations,' endowed by kings, and resorted to by the flower of the national youth, Oxford is always elegant and even splendid in her habits. Yet, on the other hand, as a grave seat of learning, and feeling the weight of her position in the commonwealth, she is slow to move: she is inert as she should be, having the functions of *resistance* assigned to her against the popular instinct of *movement*. Now, in Oxford, about 1804–5, there was a general move in the dinner hour. Those colleges who dined at three, of which there were still several, now dined at four: those who had dined at four, now translated their hour to five. These continued good general hours, but still amongst the more intellectual orders, till about Waterloo. After that era, six, which had been somewhat of a gala hour, was promoted to the fixed station of dinner-time in ordinary ; and there perhaps it will rest through centuries. For a more festal dinner, seven, eight, nine, ten, have all been in requisition since then ; but we have not yet heard of any man's dining later than 10, P. M., except in that single classical instance (so well remembered from our father Joe) of an Irishman who must have dined *much* later than ten, because his servant protested, when others were enforcing the dignity of their masters by the lateness of their dinner hours, that *his* master dined 'to-morrow.'

Were the Romans not as barbarous as our own ancestors at one time ? Most certainly they were ; in their primitive ages they took their *cœna* at noon,[12] *that* was before they had laid aside their barbarism ; before they shaved : it was during their barbarism, and in consequence of their barbarism, that they timed their *cœna* thus unseasonably. And this is made evident by the fact, that, so long as they erred in the hour, they erred in the attending circumstances. At this period they had no music at dinner, no festal graces, and no reposing upon sofas. They sate bolt upright in chairs, and were as grave as our ancestors, as rabid, and doubtless as furiously in haste.

With us the revolution has been equally complex. We do not, indeed, adopt the luxurious attitude of semi-recumbency ; our climate makes that less requisite ; and, moreover, the Romans had no knives and forks, which could scarcely be used in that posture: they ate with their fingers from dishes already cut up — whence the peculiar force of Seneca's 'post quod non sunt lavandæ manus.' But exactly in proportion as our dinner has advanced towards evening, have we and has that advanced in circumstances of elegance, of taste, of intellectual value. That by itself would be much. Infinite would be the gain for any people that it had ceased to be brutal, animal, fleshly; ceased to regard the chief meal of the day as a ministration only to an animal necessity; that they had raised it to a far higher standard; associated it with social and humanizing feelings, with manners, with graces both moral and intellectual; moral in the self-restraint; intellectual in the fact, notorious to all men, that the chief arenas for the *easy* display of intellectual power are at our dinner tables. But dinner has *now* even a greater function than this; as the fervor of our day's business increases, dinner is continually more needed in its office of a great *reaction*. We repeat that, at this moment, but for the daily relief of dinner, the brain of all men who mix in the strife of capitals would be unhinged and thrown off its centre.

If we should suppose the case of a nation taking three equidistant meals, all of the same material and the same quantity, all milk, for instance, it would be impossible for Thomas Aquinas himself to say which was or was not dinner. The case would be that of the Roman *ancile* which dropped from the skies; to prevent its ever being stolen, the priests made eleven *fac-similes* of it, that the thief, seeing the hopelessness of distinguishing the true one, might let all alone. And the result was, that, in the next generation, nobody could point to the true one. But our dinner, the Roman *cœna*, is distinguished from the rest by far more than the hour; it is distinguished by great functions, and by still greater capacities. It *is* most beneficial; it may become more so.

In saying this, we point to the lighter graces of music, and conversation *more varied*, by which the Roman *cœna* was chiefly distinguished from our dinner. We are far from agreeing with Mr. Croly, that the Roman meal was more 'intellectual' than ours. On the contrary, ours is the more intellectual by much; we have far greater knowledge, far greater means for making it such. In fact, the fault of our meal is — that it is *too* intellectual; of too severe a character; too political; too much tending, in many hands, to disquisition. Reciprocation of question and answer, variety of topics, shifting of topics, are points not sufficiently cultivated. In all else we assent to the following passage from Mr. Croly's eloquent Salathiel: —

'If an ancient Roman could start from his slumber into the midst of European life, he must look with scorn on its absence of grace, elegance, and fancy. But it is in its festivity, and most of all in its banquets, that he would feel the incurable barbarism of the Gothic blood. Contrasted with the fine displays that made the table of the Roman noble a picture, and threw over the indulgence of appetite the colors of the imagination, with what eyes must he contemplate the tasteless and commonplace dress, the coarse attendants, the meagre ornament, the want of mirth, music, and intellectual interest — the whole heavy machinery that converts the feast into the mere drudgery of devouring!'

Thus far the reader knows already that we dissent violently ; and by looking back he will see a picture of our ancestors at dinner, in which they rehearse the very part in relation to ourselves, that Mr. Croly supposes all moderns to rehearse in relation to the Romans; but in the rest of the beautiful description, the positive, though not the comparative part, we must all concur : —

'The guests before me were fifty or sixty splendidly dressed men,' (they were in fact Titus and his staff, then occupied with the siege of Jerusalem,) 'attended by a crowd of domestics, attired with scarcely less splendor ; for no man thought of coming to the banquet in the robes of ordinary life. The embroidered couches, themselves striking objects, allowed the ease of position at once delightful in the relaxing climates of the South, and capable of combining with every grace of the human figure. At a slight distance, the table loaded with plate glittering under a profusion of lamps, and surrounded by couches thus covered by rich draperies, was like a central source of light radiating in broad shafts of every brilliant hue. The wealth of the patricians, and their intercourse with the Greeks, made them masters of the first performances of the arts. Copies of the most famous statues, and groups of sculpture in the precious metals; trophies of victories; models of temples ; were mingled with vases of flowers and lighted perfumes. Finally, covering and closing all, was a vast scarlet canopy, which combined the groups beneath to the eye, and threw the whole into the form that a painter would love.'

Mr. Croly then goes on to insist on the intellectual embellishments of the Roman dinner; their variety, their grace, their adaptation to a festive purpose. The truth is, our English imagination, more profound than the Roman, is also more gloomy, less gay, less *riante*. That accounts for our want of the gorgeous *triclinium*, with its scarlet draperies, and for many other differences both to the eye and to the understanding. But both we and the Romans agree in the main point; we both discovered the true purpose which dinner might serve — 1, to throw the grace of intellectual enjoyment over an animal necessity; 2, to relieve and antagonize the toil of brain incident to high forms of social life.

Our object has been to point the eye to this fact; to show uses imperfectly suspected in a recurring accident of life; to show a steady tendency to that consummation, by holding up, as in a mirror, (together with occasional glimpses of hidden corners in history,) the corresponding revolution silently going on in a great people of antiquity.

NOTES.

Note 1. Page 210.

'In procinct.'— Milton's translation (somewhere in The Paradise Regained) of the technical phrase 'in procinctu.'

Note 2. Page 211.

'Geologists know not.' — Observe, reader, we are not at all questioning the Scriptural Chronology of the earth *as a habitation for man,* for on the pre-human earth Scripture is silent: not upon the six thousand years does our doubt revolve, but upon a very different thing, viz., to what age in man these six thousand years correspond by analogy in a planet. In man the sixtieth part is a very venerable age. But as to a planet, as to our little earth, instead of arguing dotage, six thousand years may have scarcely carried her beyond babyhood. Some people think she is cutting her first teeth; some think her in her teens. But, seriously, it is a very interesting problem. Do the sixty centuries of our earth imply youth, maturity, or dotage?

Note 3. Page 212.

'Everywhere the ancients went to bed, like good boys, from seven to nine o'clock.' — As we are perfectly serious, we must beg the reader, who fancies any joke in all this, to consider what an immense difference it must have made to the earth, considered as a steward of her own resources — whether great nations, in

a period when their resources were so feebly developed, did, or did not, for many centuries, require candles; and, we may add, fire. The five heads of human expenditure are, — 1, Food; 2, Shelter; 3, Clothing; 4, Fuel; 5, Light. All were pitched on a lower scale in the Pagan era; and the two last were almost banished from ancient housekeeping. What a great relief this must have been to our good mother the earth! who, at *first*, was obliged to request of her children that they would settle round the Mediterranean. She could not even afford them water, unless they would come and fetch it themselves out of a common tank or cistern.

NOTE 4. Page 213.

'*The mane salutantes.*'— There can be no doubt that the *levees* of modern princes and ministers have been inherited from this ancient usage of Rome; one which belonged to Rome republican, as well as Rome imperial. The fiction in our modern practice is — that we wait upon the *levé*, or rising of the prince. In France, at one era, this fiction was realized: the courtiers did really attend the king's dressing. And, as to the queen, even up to the revolution, Marie Antoinette almost from necessity gave audience at her toilette.

NOTE 5. Page 217.

'*Or again, "siccum pro biscocto, ut hodie vocamus, sumemus?"*' — It is odd enough that a scholar so complete as Salmasius, whom nothing ever escapes, should have overlooked so obvious an alternative as that of *siccus*, meaning without *opsonium* — *Scoticè*, without 'kitchen.'

NOTE 6. Page 219.

'*The whole amount of relief;*' — from which it appears how grossly Locke (see his *Education*) was deceived in fancying that Augustus practised any remarkable abstinence in taking only a bit of bread and a raisin or two, by way of luncheon. Augustus did no more than most people did; secondly, he abstained only with a view to dinner; and, thirdly, for this dinner he never waited longer than up to four o'clock.

Note 7. Page 225.

'*Mansiones.*'—The halts of the Roman legions, the stationary places of repose which divided the marches, were so called.

Note 8. Page 229.

'*The everlasting Jew;*'—the German name for what we English call the Wandering Jew. The German imagination has been most struck with the duration of the man's life, and his unhappy sanctity from death; the English by the unrestingness of the man's life, his incapacity of repose.

Note 9. Page 235.

'*Immeasurable toga.*'—It is very true that in the time of Augustus the *toga* had disappeared amongst the lowest plebs, and greatly Augustus was shocked at that spectacle. It is a very curious fact in itself, especially as expounding the main cause of the civil wars. Mere poverty, and the absence of bribery from Rome, whilst all popular competition for offices drooped, can alone explain this remarkable revolution of dress.

Note 10. Page 237.

That boys in the Prætexta did not bathe in the public baths, is certain: and most unquestionably that is the meaning of the expression in Juvenal so much disputed—'Nisi qui nondum *ære* lavantur.' By *æs* he means the *ahenum*, a common name for the public bath, which was made of copper; in our navy, 'the *coppers*' is a name for the boilers. 'Nobody believes in such tales except children,' is the meaning. This one exclusion cut off three eighths of the Roman males.

Note 11. Page 243.

'*His young English bride.*'—The case of an old man, or one reputed old, marrying a very girlish wife, is always too much for the gravity of history; and, rather than lose the joke, the historian prudently disguises the age, which, after all, was little above fifty. And the very persons who insist on the late dinner as the proximate cause of death, elsewhere insinuate something else, not so decorously expressed. It is odd that this amiable prince, so memorable as having been a martyr to late dining at eleven, A. M., was the same person who is so equally memorable for the noble answer about a King of France not remembering the wrongs of a Duke of Orleans.

NOTE 12. Page 246.

'*Took their cœna at noon.*' — And, by the way, in order to show how little *cœna* had to do with any evening hour (though, in any age but that of our fathers, four in the afternoon would never have been thought an evening hour in the sense implied by *supper*,) — the Roman *gourmands* and *bons vivants* continued through the very last ages of Rome to take their *cœna*, when more than usually sumptuous, at noon. This, indeed, all people did occasionally, just as we sometimes give a dinner even now so early as four, P. M., under the name of a *dejeuner à la fourchette*. Those who took their *cœna* so early as this, were said *de die cœnare* — to begin dining from high day. Just as the line in Horace — 'Ut jugulent homines surgunt *de nocte*, latrones,' does not mean that the robbers rise when others are going to bed, viz., at nightfall, but at midnight. For, says one of the three best scholars of this earth, *de die*, *de nocte*, mean from that hour which was most fully, most intensely day or night, viz., the centre, the meridian. This one fact is surely a clencher as to the question whether *cœna* meant dinner or supper.

ORTHOGRAPHIC MUTINEERS.

WITH A SPECIAL REFERENCE TO THE WORKS OF WALTER SAVAGE LANDOR.

As we are all of us crazy when the wind sits in some particular quarter, let not Mr. Landor be angry with me for suggesting that he is outrageously crazy upon the one solitary subject of spelling. It occurs to me, as a plausible solution of his fury upon this point, that perhaps in his earliest school-days, when it is understood that he was exceedingly pugnacious, he may have detested spelling, and (like Roberte the Deville[1]) have found it more satisfactory for all parties, that when the presumptuous schoolmaster differed from him on the spelling of a word, the question between them should be settled by a stand-up fight. Both parties would have the victory at times: and if, according to Pope's expression, 'justice rul'd the ball,' the schoolmaster (who is always a villain) would be floored three times out of four; no great matter whether wrong or not upon the immediate point of spelling discussed. It is in this way, viz., from the irregular adjudications upon litigated spelling, which must have arisen under such a mode of investigating the matter, that we account for Mr. Landor's being sometimes in the right, but too often (with regard to long words) egregiously in the wrong. As he grew stronger and taller, he would be coming more and more amongst polysyllables, and more and more would be getting the upper hand of the schoolmaster; so that at length he would have it all his own way; one round would decide the turn-up; and thenceforwards his spelling would become frightful. Now, I myself detested spelling as much as all people ought to do, except Continental compositors, who have extra fees for doctoring the lame spelling of ladies and gentlemen. But, unhappily, I had no power to thump the schoolmaster into a conviction of his own absurdities; which, however, I greatly desired to do. Still, my nature, powerless at that time for any active recusancy, was strong for passive resistance; and *that* is the hardest to conquer. I took one lesson of this infernal art, and then declined ever to take a second; and, in fact, I never *did*. Well I remember that unique morning's experience. It was the first page of Entick's Dictionary that I had to get by heart; a sweet sentimental task; and not, as may be fancied, the spelling only, but the horrid attempts of this depraved Entick to explain the supposed meaning of words that probably had none; many of these, it is my belief, Entick himself forged. Among the strange, grim-looking words, to whose acquaintance I was introduced on that unhappy morning, were *abalienate* and *ablaqueation* — most respectable words, I am fully persuaded, but so exceedingly retired in their habits, that I never once had the honor of meeting either of them in any book, pamphlet, journal, whether in prose or numerous verse, though haunting such society myself all my life. I also formed the acquaintance, at that time, of the word *abacus*, which, as a Latin word, I have often used, but, as an English one, I really never had occasion to spell, until this very moment. Yet, after all, what harm comes of such obstinate recusancy against orthography? I was an 'occasional conformist;' I conformed for one morning, and never more. But, for all that, I spell as well as my neighbors; and I can spell *ablaqueation* besides, which I suspect that some of them can *not*.

My own spelling, therefore, went right, because I was left to nature, with strict neutrality on the part of the authorities. Mr. Landor's too often went wrong, because he was thrown into a perverse channel by his continued triumphs over the prostrate schoolmaster. To toss up, as it were, for the spelling of a word, by the best of nine rounds, inevitably left the impression that chance governed all; and this accounts for the extreme capriciousness of Landor.

It is a work for a separate dictionary in quarto to record *all* the proposed revolutions in spelling, through which our English blood, either at home or in America, has thrown off, at times, the surplus energy that consumed it. I conceive this to be a sort of cutaneous affection, like nettle-rash, or ring-worm, through which the patient gains relief for his own nervous distraction, whilst, in fact, he does no harm to anybody: for usually he forgets his own reforms, and if *he* should not, everybody else *does*. Not to travel back into the seventeenth century, and the noble army of short-hand writers who have all made war upon orthography, for secret purposes of their own, even in the last century, and in the present, what a list of eminent rebels against the spelling-book might be called up to answer for their wickedness at the bar of the Old Bailey, if anybody would be kind enough to make it a felony! Cowper, for instance, too modest and too pensive to raise upon any subject an open standard of rebellion, yet, in quiet Olney, made a small *émeute* as to the word 'Grecian.' Everybody else was content with one '*e;*' but he, recollecting the cornucopia of *e*s, which Providence had thought fit to empty upon the mother word *Greece*, deemed it shocking to disinherit the poor child of its hereditary wealth, and wrote it, therefore, *Greecian* throughout his Homer. Such a modest reform the sternest old Tory could not find in his heart to denounce. But some contagion must have collected about this word *Greece;* for the next man, who had much occasion to use it — viz., Mitford[2] — who wrote that 'History of Greece' so eccentric, and so eccentrically praised by Lord Byron, absolutely took to spelling like a heathen, slashed right and left against decent old English words, until, in fact, the whole of Entick's Dictionary (*ablaqueation* and all) was ready to swear the peace against him. Mitford, in course of time, slept with his fathers; his grave, I trust, not haunted by the injured words whom he had tomahawked; and, at this present moment, the Bishop of St. David's reigneth in his stead. His Lordship, bound over to episcopal decorum, has hitherto been sparing in his assaults upon pure old English words:

but one may trace the insurrectionary taint, passing down from Cowper through the word *Grecian*, in many of his Anglo-Hellenic forms. For instance, he insists on our saying — not *Heracleidæ* and *Pelopidæ*, as we all used to do — but *Heracleids* and *Pelopids*. A list of my Lord's barbarities, in many other cases, upon unprotected words, poor shivering aliens that fall into his power, when thrown upon the coast of his diocese, I had — *had*, I say, for, alas! *fuit Ilium*.

Yet, really, one is ashamed to linger on cases so mild as those, coming, as one does, in the order of atrocity, to Elphinstone, to Noah Webster, a Yankee — which word means, not an American, but that separate order of Americans, growing in Massachusetts, Rhode Island, or Connecticut, in fact, a New Englander[3] — and to the rabid Ritson. Noah would naturally have reduced us all to an antediluvian simplicity. Shem, Ham, and Japhet, probably separated in consequence of perverse varieties in spelling; so that orthographical unity might seem to him one condition for preventing national schisms. But as to the rabid Ritson, who can describe his vagaries? What great arithmetician can furnish an index to his absurdities, or what great decipherer furnish a key to the principles of these absurdities? In his very title-pages, nay, in the most obstinate of ancient technicalities, he showed his cloven foot to the astonished reader. Some of his many works were printed in *Pall-Mall;* now, as the world is pleased to pronounce that word *Pel-Mel*, thus and no otherwise (said Ritson) it shall be spelled for ever. Whereas, on the contrary, some men would have said: The spelling is well enough, it is the public pronunciation which is wrong. This ought to be *Paul-Maul;* or, perhaps — agreeably to the sound which we give to the *a* in such words as *what*, *quantity*, *want* — still better, and with more gallantry, *Poll-Moll.* The word Mr., again, in Ritson's reformation, must have astonished the Post-office. He insisted that this cabalistical-looking form, which might as reasonably be translated into *monster*, was a direct fraud on the national language, quite as bad as clipping the Queen's coinage. How, then, *should* it be written? Reader! reader! that you will ask such a question! *mister*, of course; and mind that you put no capital *m;* unless, indeed, you are speaking of some great gun, some mister of misters, such as Mr. Pitt of old, or perhaps a reformer of spelling. The plural, again, of such words as *romance*, *age*, *horse*, he wrote *romanceës*, *ageës*, *horseës;* and upon the following equitable consideration, that, inasmuch as the *e* final in the singular is mute, that is, by a general vote of the nation has been allowed to retire upon a superannuation allowance, it is abominable to call it back upon active service — like the modern Chelsea pensioners — as must be done, if it is to bear the whole weight of a separate syllable like *ces.* Consequently, if the nation and Parliament mean to keep faith, they are bound to hire a stout young *e* to run in the traces with the old original *e*, taking the whole work off his aged shoulders. Volumes would not suffice to exhaust the madness of Ritson upon this subject. And there was this peculiarity in his madness, over and above its clamorous ferocity, that being no classical scholar, (a meagre self-taught Latinist, and no Grecian at all,) though profound as a black-letter scholar, he cared not one straw for ethnographic relations of words, nor for unity of analogy, which are the principles that generally have governed reformers of spelling. He was an attorney, and moved constantly under the *monomaniac* idea that an action lay on behalf of misused letters, mutes, liquids, vowels, and diphthongs, against somebody or other (John Doe, was it, or Richard Roe ?) for trespass on any rights of theirs which an attorney might trace, and of course for any direct outrage upon their persons. Yet no man was more systematically an offender in both ways than himself; tying up one leg of a quadruped word, and forcing it to run upon three ; cutting off noses and ears, if he fanced that equity required it : and living in eternal hot water with a language which he pretended eternally to protect.

And yet all these fellows were nothing in comparison of Mr.[4] Pinkerton. The most of these men did but ruin the national *spelling;* but Pinkerton — the monster Pinkerton — proposed a revolution which would have left us nothing to spell. It is almost incredible — if a book regularly printed and published, bought and sold, did not remain to attest the fact — that this horrid barbarian seriously proposed, as a glorious discovery for refining our language, the following plan. All people were content with the compass of the English language : its range of expression was equal to anything ; but, unfortunately, as compared with the sweet orchestral languages of the south — Spanish the stately, and Italian the lovely — it wanted rhythmus and melody. Clearly, then, the one supplementary grace, which it remained for modern art to give, is that every one should add at discretion *o* and *a*, *ino* and *ano*, to the end of the English words. The language, in its old days, should be taught *struttare struttissimamente.* As a specimen, Mr. Pinkerton favored us with his own version of a famous passage in Addison, viz., 'The Vision of Mirza.' The passage, which begins thus, 'As I sat on the top of a rock,' being translated into, 'As I satto on the toppino of a rocko,' &c. But *luckilissime* this *proposalio* of the *absurdissimo Pinkertonio*[5] was not *adoptado* by *anybody-ini whatever-ano.*

Mr. Landor is more learned, and probably more consistent in his assaults upon the established spelling than most of these elder reformers. But *that* does not make him either learned enough or consistent enough. He never ascends into Anglo-Saxon, or the many cognate languages of the Teutonic family, which is indispensable to a searching inquest upon our language; he does not put forward in this direction even the slender qualifications of Horne Tooke. But Greek and Latin are quite unequal, when disjoined from the elder wheels in our etymological system, to the working of the total machinery of the English language. Mr. Landor proceeds upon no fixed principles in his changes. Sometimes it is on the principle of internal analogy with itself, that he would distort or retrotort the language; sometimes on the principle of external analogy with its roots; sometimes on the principle of euphony, or of metrical convenience. Even within such principles he is not uniform. All well-built English scholars, for instance, know that the word *feälty* cannot be made into a dissyllable: trissyllabic it ever was[6] with the elder poets — Spenser, Milton, &c.; and so it is amongst all the modern poets who have taken any pains with their English studies: *e.g.*

> 'The eagle, lord of land and sea,
> Stoop'd down — to pay him fe-al-ty.'

It is dreadful to hear a man say *feal-ty* in any case; but here it is luckily impossible. Now, Mr. Landor generally is correct, and trisects the word; but once, at least, he bisects it. I complain, besides, that Mr. Landor, in urging the authority of Milton for orthographic innovations, does not always distinguish as to Milton's motives. It is true, as he contends, that, in some instances, Milton reformed the spelling in obedience to the Italian precedent: and certainly without blame; as in *sovran*, *sdeign*, which ought not to be printed (as it is) with an elision before the *s*, as if short for disdain; but in other instances Milton's motive had no reference to etymology. Sometimes it was this. In Milton's day, the modern use of italics was nearly unknown. Everybody is aware that, in our authorized version of the Bible, published in Milton's infancy, italics are never once used for the purpose of emphasis — but exclusively to indicate such words or auxiliary forms as, though implied and *virtually* present in the original, are not textually expressed, but must be so in English, from the different genius of the language.[7] Now, this want of a proper technical resource amongst the compositors of the age, for indicating a peculiar stress upon a word, evidently drove Milton into some perplexity for a compensatory contrivance. It was unusually requisite for *him*, with his elaborate metrical system and his divine ear, to have an art for throwing attention upon his accents, and upon his muffling of accents. When, for instance, he wishes to direct a bright jet of emphasis upon the possessive pronoun *their*, he writes it as we now write it. But, when he wishes to take off the accent, he writes it *thir*.[8] Like Ritson, he writes *therefor* and *wherefor* without the final *e;* not regarding the analogy, but singly the metrical quantity: for it was shocking to his classical feeling that a sound so short to the ear should be represented to the eye by so long a combination as *fore;* and the more so, because uneducated people did then, and do now, often equilibrate the accent between the two syllables, or rather make the *quantity* long in both syllables, whilst giving an over-balance of the *accent* to the last. The 'Paradise Lost,' being printed during Milton's blindness, did not receive the full and consistent benefit of his spelling reforms, which (as I have contended) certainly arose partly in the imperfections of typography at that æra: but such changes as had happened most to impress his ear with a sense of their importance, he took a special trouble, even under all the disadvantages of his darkness, to have rigorously adopted. He must have astonished the compositors, though not quite so much as the tiger-cat Ritson or the Mr. (viz. monster) Pinkerton — each after *his* kind — astonished *their* compositors.

But the caprice of Mr. Landor is shown most of all upon Greek names. *Nous autres* say 'Aristotle,' and are quite content with it, until we migrate into some extra-superfine world; but this title will not do for *him:* 'Aristotles' it must be. And why so? Because, answers the Landor, if once I consent to say Aristotle, then I am pledged to go the whole hog; and perhaps the next man I meet is Empedocles, whom, in that case, I must call Empedocle. Well, do so. *Call* him Empedocle; it will not break his back, which seems broad enough. But, now, mark the contradictions in which Mr. Landor is soon landed. He says, as everybody says, Terence, and not Terentius, Horace and not Horatius; but he must leave off such horrid practices, because he dares not call Lucretius by the analogous name of Lucrece, since *that* would be putting a she instead of a he; nor Propertius by the name of Properce, because *that* would be speaking French instead of English. Next he says, and continually he says, Virgil for Virgilius. But, on that principle, he ought to say Valer for Valerius; and yet again he ought *not:* because, as he says Tully and not Tull for Tullius, so also is he bound, in Christian equity, to say Valery for Valer; but he cannot say either Valer or Valery. So here we are in a mess. Thirdly, I charge him with saying Ovid for Ovidius: which *I* do, which everybody does, but which *he* must not do: for, if he means to persist in *that*, then, upon his own argument from analogy, he must call Didius Julianus by the shocking name of *Did*, which is the same thing as Tit — since T is D soft. Did was a very great man indeed, and for a very short time indeed. Probably Did was the only man that ever bade for an empire, and no mistake, at a public auction. Think of Did's bidding for the Roman empire: nay, think also of Did's having the lot actually knocked down to him ; and of Did's going home to dinner with the lot in his pocket. It makes one perspire to think that, if the reader or myself had been living at that time, and had been prompted by some whim within us to bid against him — that is, he or I — should actually have come down to posterity by the abominable name of Anti-Did. All of us in England say Livy when speaking of the great historian, not Livius. Yet Livius Andronicus it would be impossible to indulge with that brotherly name of Livy. Marcus Antonius is called — not by Shakspeare only, but by all the world — Mark Antony ; but who is it that ever called Marcus Brutus by the affectionate name of Mark Brute ? 'Keep your distance,' we say, to that very doubtful brute, 'and expect no pet names from us.' Finally, apply the principle of abbreviation, involved in the names Pliny, Livy, Tully, all substituting *y* for *ius*, to Marius — that grimmest of grim visions that rises up to us from the phantasmagoria of Roman history. Figure to yourself, reader, that truculent face, trenched and scarred with hostile swords, carrying thunder in its ominous eye-brows, and frightening armies a mile off with its scowl, being saluted by the tenderest of feminine names, as 'My Mary.'

Not only, therefore, is Mr. Landor inconsistent in these innovations, but the innovations themselves, supposing them all harmonized and established, would but plough up the landmarks of old hereditary feelings. We learn oftentimes, by a man's bearing a good-natured sobriquet amongst his comrades, that he is a kind-hearted, social creature, popular with them all ! And it is an illustration of the same tendency, that the scale of popularity for the classical authors amongst our fathers, is registered tolerably well, in a gross general way, by the difference between having and *not* having a familiar name. If we except the first Cæsar, the mighty Caius Julius, who was too majestic to invite familiarity, though too gracious to have repelled it, there is no author whom our forefathers loved, but has won a sort of Christian name in the land. Homer, and Hesiod, and Pindar, we all say; we cancel the alien *us;* but we never say Theocrit for Theocritus. Anacreon remains rigidly Grecian marble; but *that* is only because his name is not of a plastic form — else everybody loves the sad old fellow. The same bar to familiarity existed in the names of the tragic poets, except perhaps for Æschylus; who, however, like Cæsar, is too awful for a caressing name. But Roman names were, generally, more flexible. Livy and Sallust have ever been favorites with men; Livy with everybody; Sallust, in a degree that may be called extravagant, with many celebrated Frenchmen, as the President des Brosses, and in our own days with M. Lerminier, a most eloquent and original writer ('*Etudes Historiques*'); and two centuries ago, with the greatest of men, John Milton, in a degree that seems to me absolutely mysterious. These writers are baptized into our society — have gained a settlement in our parish; when you call a man Jack, and not Mr. John, it's plain you like him. But, as to the gloomy Tacitus, our fathers liked him not. He was too vinegar a fellow for them; nothing hearty or genial about him; he thought ill of everybody; and we all suspect that, for those times, he was perhaps the worst of the bunch himself. Accordingly, this Tacitus, because he remained so perfectly tacit for our jolly old forefathers' ears, never slipped into the name Tacit for their mouths; nor ever will, I predict, for the mouths of posterity. Coming to the Roman poets, I must grant that three great ones, viz., Lucretius, Statius, and Valerius Flaccus, have not been complimented with the freedom of our city, as they should have been, in a gold box. I regret, also, the ill fortune, in this respect, of Catullus, if he was really the author of that grand headlong dithyrambic, the Atys: he certainly ought to have been ennobled by the title of Catull. Looking to very much of his writings, much more I regret the case of Plautus: and I am sure that if her Majesty would warrant his bearing the name and arms of *Plaut* in all time coming, it would gratify many of us. As to the rest, or those that anybody cares about, Horace, Virgil, Ovid, Lucan, Martial, Claudian, all have been raised to the peerage. Ovid was the great poetic favorite of Milton; and not without a philosophic ground: his festal gaiety, and the brilliant velocity of his *aurora borealis* intellect, forming a deep natural equipoise to the mighty gloom and solemn planetary movement in the mind of the other; like the wedding of male and female counterparts. Ovid was, therefore, rightly Milton's favorite. But the favorite of all the world is Horace. Were there ten peerages, were there three blue ribbons, vacant, he ought to have them all.

Besides, if Mr. Landor could issue decrees, and even harmonize his decrees for reforming our Anglo-Grecian spelling — decrees which no Council of Trent could execute, without first rebuilding the Holy office of the Inquisition — still there would be little accomplished. The names of all continental Europe are often in confusion, from different causes, when Anglicised: German names are rarely spelled rightly by the *laity* of our isle: Polish and Hungarian never. Many foreign towns have in England what botanists would call *trivial* names; Leghorn, for instance, Florence, Madrid, Lisbon, Vienna, Munich, Antwerp, Brussels, the Hague — all unintelligible names to the savage Continental native. Then, if Mr. Landor reads as much of Anglo-Indian books as I do, he must be aware that, for many years back, they have all been at sixes and sevens; so that now most Hindoo words are in masquerade, and we shall soon require *English* pundits in Leadenhall Street.[9] How does he like, for instance, *Sipahee* the modern form for *Sepoy*? or *Tepheen* for *Tiffin*? At this rate of metamorphosis, absorbing even the consecrated names of social meals, we shall soon cease to understand what that *disjune* was which his sacred Majesty graciously accepted at Tillietudlem. But even elder forms of oriental speech are as little harmonized in Christendom. A few leagues of travelling make the Hebrew unintelligible to us; and the Bible becomes a Delphic mystery to Englishmen amongst the countrymen of Luther. Solomon is there called Salamo; Samson is called Simson, though probably he never published an edition of Euclid. Nay, even in this native isle of ours, you may be at cross purposes on the Bible with your own brother. I am, myself, next door neighbor to Westmoreland, being a Lancashire man; and, one day, I was talking with a

Westmoreland farmer, whom, of course, I ought to have understood very well; but I had no chance with him: for I could not make out who that *No* was, concerning *whom* or concerning *which*, he persisted in talking. It seemed to me, from the context, that *No* must be a man, and by no means a chair; but so very negative a name, you perceive, furnished no positive hints for solving the problem. I said as much to the farmer, who stared in stupefaction. 'What,' cried he, 'did a far-larn'd man, like you, fresh from Oxford, never hear of *No*, an old gentleman that should have been drowned, but was *not*, when all his folk were drowned?' 'Never, so help me Jupiter,' was my reply: 'never heard of him to this hour, any more than of *Yes*, an old gentleman that should have been hanged, but was *not*, when all his folk were hanged. *Populous No* — I had read of in the Prophets; but that was *not* an old gentleman.' It turned out that the farmer and all his compatriots in bonny Martindale had been taught at the parish school to rob the Patriarch Noah of one clear moiety appertaining in fee simple to that ancient name. But afterwards I found that the farmer was not so entirely absurd as he had seemed. The Septuagint, indeed, is clearly against him; for *there*, as plain as a pike-staff, the farmer might have read Νωε̈. But, on the other hand, Pope, not quite so great a scholar as he was a poet, yet still a fair one, *always* made Noah into a monosyllable; and that seems to argue an old English usage; though I really believe Pope's reason for adhering to such an absurdity was with a prospective view to the rhymes *blow*, or *row*, or *stow*, (an important idea to the Ark) which struck him as *likely* words, in case of any call for writing about Noah.

The long and the short of it is — that the whole world lies in heresy or schism on the subject of orthography. All climates alike groan under heterography. It is absolutely of no use to begin with one's own grandmother in such labors of reformation. It is toil thrown away: and as nearly hopeless a task as the proverb insinuates that it is to attempt a reformation in that old lady's mode of eating eggs. She laughs at one. She has a vain conceit that she is able, out of her own proper resources, to do both, viz., the spelling and the eating of the eggs. And all that remains for philosophers, like Mr. Landor and myself, is — to turn away in sorrow rather than in anger, dropping a silent tear for the poor old lady's infatuation.

NOTES.

NOTE 1. Page 255.

'*Roberte the Deville:*' — See the old metrical romance of that name: it belongs to the fourteenth century, and was printed some thirty years ago, with wood engravings of the illuminations. Roberte, however, took the liberty of murdering *his* schoolmaster. But could he well do less? Being a reigning Duke's son, and after the rebellious schoolmaster had said —

'Sir, ye bee too bolde:
And therewith tooke a rodde hym for to chaste.'

Upon which the meek Robin, without using any bad language as the schoolmaster had done, simply took out a long dagger '*hym for to chaste,*' which he did effectually. The schoolmaster gave no bad language after that.

NOTE 2. Page 258.

Mitford, who was the brother of a man better known than himself to the public eye, viz., Lord Redesdale, may be considered a very unfortunate author. His work upon Greece, which Lord Byron celebrated for its 'wrath and its partiality,' really had those merits: choleric it was in excess, and as entirely partial, as nearly perfect in its injustice, as human infirmity would allow. Nothing is truly perfect in this shocking world; absolute injustice, alas! the perfection of wrong, must not be looked for until we reach some high Platonic form of polity. Then shall we revel and bask in a vertical sun of iniquity. Meantime, I *will* say — that to satisfy all bilious and unreasonable men, a better historian of Greece, than Mitford, could not be fancied. And yet, at the very moment when he was stepping into his harvest of popularity, down comes one of those omnivorous Germans that, by reading everything, and a trifle besides, contrive to throw really learned men — and perhaps better thinkers than themselves — into the shade. Ottfried Mueller, with other archæologists and travellers into Hellas, gave new aspects to the very purposes of Grecian history. Do you hear, reader? not new answers, but new questions. And Mitford, that was gradually displacing the unlearned Gillies, &c., was himself displaced by those who intrigued with Germany. His other work on 'the Harmony of Language,' though one of the many that attempted, and the few that accomplished, the distinction between accent and quantity, or learnedly appreciated the metrical science of Milton, was yet, in my hearing, pronounced utterly intelligible, by the best *practical* commentator on Milton, viz., the best reproducer of his exquisite effects in blank verse, that any generation since Milton has been able to show. Mr. Mitford was one of the many accomplished scholars that are ill-used. Had he possessed the splendid powers of the Landor, he would have raised a clatter on the armor of modern society, such as Samson threatened to the giant Harapha. For, in many respects, he resembled the Landor: he had much of his learning — he had the same extensive access to books and influential circles in great cities — the same gloomy disdain of popular falsehoods or common-places — and the same disposition to run a muck against all nations, languages, and spelling-books.

NOTE 3. Page 259.

'In fact, a New Englander.' — This explanation, upon a matter familiar to the well-informed, it is proper to repeat occasionally, because we English exceedingly perplex and

confound the Americans by calling, for instance, a Virginian or a Kentuck by the name of Yankee, whilst that term was originally introduced as antithetic to these more southern States.

NOTE 4. Page 261.

Pinkerton published one of his earliest volumes, under this title — 'Rimes, by Mr. Pinkerton,' not having the fear of Ritson before his eyes. And, for once, we have reason to thank Ritson for his remark — that the form Mr. might just as well be read *Monster*. Pinkerton in this point was a perfect monster. As to the word *Rimes*, instead of *Rhymes*, he had something to stand upon ; the Greek *rythmos* was certainly the remote fountain ; but the proximate fountain must have been the Italian *rima*.

NOTE 5. Page 262.

The most extravagant of all experiments on language is brought forward in the '*Letters of Literature*, by Robert Heron.' But Robert Heron is a *pseudonyme* for John Pinkerton ; and I have been told that Pinkerton's motive for assuming it was — because *Heron* had been the maiden name of his mother. Poor lady, she would have stared to find herself, in old age, transformed into Mistressina Heronilla. What most amuses one in pursuing the steps of such an attempt at refinement, is its reception by 'Jack' in the navy.

NOTE 6. Page 263.

'*It ever was*' — and, of course, being (as there is no need to tell Mr. Landor) a form obtained by contraction from *fidelitas*.

NOTE 7. Page 263.

Of this a ludicrous illustration is mentioned by the writer once known to the public as *Trinity Jones*. Some young clergyman, unacquainted with the technical use of italics by the original compositors of James the First's Bible, on coming to the 27th verse, chap. xiii. of 1st Kings, 'And he' (viz. the old prophet of Bethel) 'spake to his sons, saying, Saddle me the ass. And they saddled *him*;' (where the italic *him* simply meant that this word was involved, but not expressed, in the original,) read it, 'And they saddled HIM;' as though these undutiful sons, instead of saddling the donkey, had saddled the old prophet. In fact, the old gentleman's directions are not quite without an opening for a filial misconception, if the reader examines them as closely as *I* examine words.

NOTE 8. Page 264.

He uses this and similar artifices, in fact, as the damper in a modern piano-forte, for modifying the swell of the intonation.

NOTE 9. Page 269.

The reasons for this anarchy in the naturalization of Eastern words are to be sought in three causes: 1. In national rivalships: French travellers in India, like Jacquemont, &c., as they will not adopt our English First Meridian, will not, of course, adopt our English spelling. In one of Paul Richter's novels a man assumes the First Meridian to lie generally, not through Greenwich, but through his own skull, and always through his own study. I have myself long suspected the Magnetic Pole to lie under a friend's wine-cellar, from the vibrating movement which I have remarked constantly going on in his cluster of keys towards that particular point. Really, the French, like Sir Anthony Absolute, must 'get an atmosphere of their own,' such is their hatred to holding anything in common with us. 2. They are to be sought in local *Indian* differences of pronunciation. 3. In the variety of our own British population — soldiers, missionaries, merchants, who are unlearned or half-learned — scholars, really learned, but often fantastically learned, and lastly (as you may swear) young ladies — anxious, above all things, to mystify us outside barbarians.

www.ingramcontent.com/pod-product-compliance
Lightning Source LLC
LaVergne TN
LVHW010231110826
845151LV00004B/1263

9781425525293